Reading Matters

The Centre for Language in Primary Education, established by the Inner London Education Authority, is concerned with in-service education for teachers in the fields of language and literacy. At the time of the writing of this book, the staff consisted of:

Moira McKenzie (Adviser/Warden)
Aidan Warlow
Ruth Ballin
Ian Forsyth
Ralph Lavender
Norris Bentham (Librarian)

Reading Matters

Selecting and using books in the classroom

Written by the staff of the Centre for Language in Primary
Education
Edited by Moira McKenzie and Aidan Warlow

Hodder and Stoughton
in association with Inner London Education Authority

94940

027.8
MAC

0126730

ISBN 0 340 22187 9

First published 1977
Copyright © 1977 Inner London Education Authority

Printed and bound in Great Britain for
Hodder and Stoughton Educational,
a division of Hodder and Stoughton Ltd,
Mill Road, Dunton Green, Sevenoaks, Kent,
by William Clowes & Sons Ltd, London, Beccles and Colchester.

Contents

Preface

Every day, teachers come to the Centre for Language in Primary Education in Sutherland Street, London SW1, to browse in the large library of children's books and to talk with Centre staff about the books they want for their particular schools or classrooms, and about ways in which children's understanding and enjoyment of books might be extended.

This book is a summary of the advice that we at the Centre have to give. Not everybody will agree with all of it. But we hope that all will acknowledge the importance of its two main principles: that in order to enable children to become readers, we must take the utmost care to supply them with the most attractive and rewarding books available; and that we must ensure that children see reading as a necessary and pleasurable activity by relating it to the general work of the classroom, to life outside school and to the inner life of the individual.

I

Why Have a Classroom Collection?

CREATING A READING ENVIRONMENT

The school has a responsibility not only to teach reading but also to create an environment that will make children want to read and will enable them to discover the excitement of reading. This presupposes an environment in which people actually read, where space and time are allowed for reading and discussing books, where reading is accepted as part of everyday life, where peer-group influence works towards reading rather than against it.

Reading to get a good story, or to check information, or to follow up an inquiry is a different kind of reading from reading just for the sake of learning to read. Many teachers make the classroom collection the basic source of reading, while others who use basic schemes find it a valuable way of extending purposeful and enjoyable reading.

If we want children to become autonomous readers who not only *can* read but *do* read independently, then they must feel there is something for them in books and in reading. The satisfactions they receive need to counter-balance the effort they put in. This means providing attractive and interesting books. What are some of the personal satisfactions that are likely to accrue?

SATISFYING THE CHILD'S NEEDS AND INTERESTS

Sheer enjoyment

Every child enjoys a good story, whether it's an anecdote heard in the playground, a serial watched on TV, a Superman comic read in bed when the lights should be out, or a novel read to the class by the teacher.

Stories meet a basic need in children. They help them to

bring together and understand what they know, and to realise what they feel. In a state of 'suspended disbelief' they can experience joy, sadness, horror, awe, laughter and fear—feelings that give pleasure. And at the same time, they are enlarging their knowledge of the world beyond their immediate experience by sharing the imagined life of the storyteller. Looked at this way, the story becomes one of the most potent of all educational instruments.

Understanding self and others

Experience of life as it is actually lived, and the satisfaction arising from recognising real life situations, is evident in books ranging from Ezra Jack Keats' *Goggles* to Bill Naughton's *The Goalkeeper's Revenge*. We may get an inkling of life elsewhere in books such as *Little House on the Prairie* by Laura Ingalls Wilder, or in Ben Butterworth's amusing TROG series about a Stone Age family. Karl Craig's *Emanuel goes to Market* gives us a picture of life in a Jamaican market and Ian Serraillier's *The Silver Sword* tells a story of suffering during the Second World War. Sometimes children's emotional life is symbolized by talking animals, as in Russell Hoban's *Frances* books about family relationships, and E. B. White's *Charlotte's Web* which deals with the growth of individuality and the discovery of death.

Children also enjoy focusing on life as they would *like* it to be. This means reading not only traditional fairy tales but also modern formula fiction of the Blyton and Buckeridge variety (holiday adventures and school life in which ideal playmates engage in desirable but unrealistic activities such as capturing smugglers and getting stranded in a lighthouse). Beyond this they need thoughtful and creative statements about alternative better worlds, as in Quentin Blake's *Patrick*, J. R. R. Tolkien's *The Hobbit,* or *Enchantress from the Stars* by S. L. Engdahl.

Learning about things that matter

For this purpose, good information books are needed—books which either spark off new interests—in cathedrals, or moths, for example—or satisfy and extend established interests such as football strategy, or cars. The best texts contain plenty of vivid, concrete, specific information: one book on big animals tells us the impressive fact that 'The tongue of a whale weighs more than a whole elephant.' Such books are for browsing as well as reading.

Satisfaction in developing one's own reading power

The collection needs to include books across a wide range of reading ability so that all children can experience the satisfaction and enjoyment of reading, sometimes sampling new books and stories, sometimes recapturing the pleasure of books already known. Some of the time they will be stretching themselves; at other times they will be reading effortlessly within their capacity. Jenkinson, in his classic survey *What do Boys and Girls Read?* (1940), pointed out:

> Children's reading matter can be classified into three sorts according to its significance for the individual: some of it is residual and derives from stages outgrown; most of it refers to the actual situation, to the stage in which the child finds himself; some of it indicates potentialities. ... The teacher's task is to satisfy the actual, to promote the potential, and to tolerate the residual, remembering ... that adults also live at many levels.

ADVANCING THE GOALS AND PURPOSES OF THE SCHOOL

The content and experience of literature

The classroom collection of books is the main resource for an important area of the curriculum. Through listening to and reading and discussing books children get the opportunity of sampling a wide range of literature, in terms of genre and theme. The range includes realistic fiction, traditional stories and fantasy; and themes that are concerned with good and evil, as in Lloyd Alexander's *The High King*; courage, as in the *Island of the Blue Dolphins* by Scott O'Dell; and loneliness, as in *The Secret Garden* by Frances Hodgson Burnett. It offers folk tales from many sources, and different versions of the same folk tale: Rumer Godden's *The Old Woman who Lived in a Vinegar Bottle* and Harve Zemach's *The Fisherman and his Wife*. It includes collections of rhymes and poetry, from *Mother Goose* and the *Puffin Joke Book* to *Junior Voices*.

As the teacher sets up a collection for a particular group of children she takes into account their age and stage of development, their experience of literature, their interests and their community setting. The goal is to give them a growing acquaintance with a wide range of literature that gives them pleasure and satisfaction, that feeds and extends their own sense of story.

The teacher shares with children the excitement and joy of reading. Through literature children gain new perspectives on things they already have some experience of. For example, the child who reads Rumer Godden's *The Diddakoi* is likely to gain new insights into what it feels like to be the odd-man-out. In the same way, Ivan Southall's *Let the Balloon Go*, which is about a spastic child's desire to be independent, latches on to something universal in all children's experience.

Through books, children can be transported to other places and into different periods of time. Through their imagination they can enter into the feelings experienced by others even if they cannot share the experience itself. For example, in the story *The Boy Who Was Afraid* by Armstrong Sperry, children will readily identify with Mafatu, who is taunted by his fellows because of his overwhelming fear of the sea. Since the story has an early Polynesian setting, where courage is worshipped, it bodes ill for the chief's son to have such fear. We share his feelings as he sets out on his own in his canoe, determined to conquer his fear:

> The boy's hands tightened on his paddle. Behind him lay safety, security from the sea. What matter if they jeered? For a second he almost turned back. Then he heard Kana's voice once more saying: "Mafatu is a coward."

> The canoe entered the race formed by the ebbing tide. It caught up the small craft in its churn, swept it forward like a chip on a mill-race. No turning back now ... (p. 13)

Lifetime habits and attitudes

A well-thought-out classroom collection of books can become a major tool for helping children acquire good attitudes to learning and the requisite skills. The teacher may use books as a way of stimulating interest and arousing curiosity for individuals or groups of children. For example, a teacher of seven-to-eight-year-olds assembled a group of books about canals as a prelude to a canal trip and as material for following it up during the rest of the school year. Many teachers place a few relevant books near collections of fossils or shells, or alongside creatures kept by the children such as frogs and toads, snakes or gerbils. They encourage the children to use these books to provide information about feeding, and habitat for example, to explain behaviour such as the hamsters' nocturnal habits, and to compare the animals' behaviour with the facts in the books. A teacher with a third year junior class who were in the habit of keeping and studying creatures in the classroom describes what followed after beginning a new term by reading William Steig's *Amos and Boris* to her class.

I chose this picture story book to begin a new term. I had enjoyed the quality of the language enormously and felt that the content was quite challenging. The story tells of a mouse who builds himself a boat which he names 'Rodent', and sets sail. Overcome by the beauty of the world beneath the stars, he falls in the sea and is rescued by a whale. He rides on the whale's back with many adventures and difficulties over food. The mouse is left safely on dry land promising to help the whale should he ever need it. Eventually the whale is in need of help and the mouse saves him. Once again they part with great respect and affection.

My group of children, all except two newcomers, were very familiar with gerbils, mice and guinea pigs. Before the story I asked what 'Rodent' meant to them. There was a good response of 'it's like a mouse, isn't it?' 'it's animals that scavenge in dustbins', 'hawks and other birds of prey eat them, don't they?'—all reflecting very personal points of view but building up the characteristics of rodent. One of the newcomers announced to a stunned audience that 'it was a mammal with its front teeth specially adapted for gnawing'.

After the story, the children spontaneously commented on the story's similarity with the *Lion and the Rat*—the Wildsmith version was known to them. They carried on discussing and listing rodents. Someone mentioned that the mouse was the smallest mammal, the whale the largest—what a funny friendship—and much more.

I talked to a new child about the gerbils. Did she think they were rodents? She didn't know. After much discussion it was clear that she had no criteria which she could use for recognising either mammals or rodents. The acquisition of features of rodents took her about six months.

Soon after this we saw the *Picture Box* film 'Journey into Spring' in which a sleepy hedgehog took his first swim. Connections were instantly made with *Amos and Boris*. Could the mouse really swim or was it a story? Is a hedgehog a rodent? In *Squirrels* (by B. Wildsmith) they swim and use their tails as rudders. The next step was obvious: all reference books were consulted, including *Animals in the Home and Classroom* (T. J. Jennings)—usually reliable—but none had this information. The guinea pigs and the gerbils were tested and swam well. Looking again at *Squirrels*, their teeth suddenly became significant—the children compared the squirrel skeleton in the *Clue Book of Bones*, with the rabbit and mouse skeletons. This aroused great excitement at the similarity. One child focused on the length of the back limbs, so evident in the skeleton photographs, and made marvellous observations of the way in which gerbils, mice, and squirrels sat up to eat their food holding it, but how the guinea pigs with significantly shorter limbs did not show this same characteristic.

Reading for different purposes

Children need to experience reading for different purposes, for a skilled reader should have a range of reading behaviours available to him to use when he reads for pleasure, or seeks information, or skims in order to pinpoint specific information.

Children using a classroom collection as an adjunct to everyday learning need to acquire this range of abilities. Having books so handy enables a teacher actively to assist the youngsters to acquire these skills 'on the run'. For example, the younger child begins his learning about dictionaries through his first teacher-made one, which is an alphabetically-arranged personal collection. He will learn that there can be more than one book on a subject. He learns how to use the table of contents to find the particular story he is looking for, and to survey the range of stories in a collection in order to find others, perhaps by the same author, or on the same subject. In a good learning situation he needs to go to many reference books. He is taught to use an index as he seeks information. He learns to survey a range of books, maybe five or six different books on the Vikings or the planets, so that he can pinpoint and compare specific information. His teachers make sure that gradually he learns how to use the table of contents, the index, and the chapter headings; how to identify important information; and how to know how to find the particular books that fulfil his purpose. He gets to know that different kinds of books give different kinds of insights and information.

When a reader is aware of what he wants to know, he poses his own questions. This is basic to real comprehension for it hinges on the background of experience the child himself brings to the reading material. Seeking answers to one's own questions is apparent in the following example of third-year juniors investigating a cuttle-fish bone they found on the beach whey they were away on a school journey. Their teacher writes:

We found a cuttle-fish bone. Back at school John carefully drew this. Then he scraped off a piece of the hard shiny surface. I know nothing about cuttle fish apart from feeding it to budgies. The index in the *Observer's Book of the Seashore* led to a section of Squids and Octopus. This was exciting but the language was not easy to understand. It

Using books to explain, verify and extend experience—in this case, a house plant.

didn't matter because it had thrown new light on the class where cuttle fish belonged.

From the library John got Black's picture information book on the sea-shore. He read the cuttle fish section at least ten times, twice to me, and each time something new fell into place. The shiny bit he had scraped off was the covering of the shell, the sort of thing you could find on any dry sea shell. It was a shell, not a bone, but it was an internal shell. What did this mean? No one knew. Someone went to the dictionary. *Internal* and *external* were talked about and gradually the cuttle shell was sorted out, and the growth marks identified. It was the first time I had come across the idea of an internal shell.

As Bullock puts it, 'To read intelligently is to read responsively; it is to ask questions of the text and use one's own framework of experience in interpreting it' (p. 129).

Magazines, newspapers and periodicals that come and go are part of the classroom collection. They provide excellent opportunity for discussion of bias and prejudice in writing, of propaganda devices, and of highly emotive writing. Try getting young football fans to read reports on a particular game written in the local papers of each side. The advertisements themselves are very suitable for reading critically, and critical reading is akin to critical thinking. The reader needs to analyse and evaluate what he is reading in order to make some kind of judgment, both about the content and the way the material is presented.

Catering for different reading abilities and interests

All teachers have to cater for a wide range of reading ability in their classes, possibly as wide as six or seven years. This means, for example, that the first year junior class may well cover a range from the very beginning stages to a reading age of twelve. Of course, we know that a young child even with high reading ability cannot understand books for which he has no experience or conceptual background, and in which he has no interest.

The capable reader will find plenty to engage him in a good collection. The slow starter must find just as much to engage him, too, if he is to become 'hooked on books'. Many of the books already mentioned can be tackled if the reader has enjoyed hearing them read aloud, for the characters and plot will already be familiar. In addition, the collection will include books from graded series that meet the criteria of good story and high interest for the child. For example, books in the STEPPING STONES range are much enjoyed by young juniors of varied reading abilities. Some of them, like *Snake in the Camp* are hilariously illustrated. Another, *A Nail, a Stick and a Lid,* will amuse because it shows Billy, who was thought by his friends to be a bit slow, as not really being at all daft! SEVEN SILLY STORIES, too, is a series which is amusingly illustrated and simply told in natural language:

The Well Diggers is a good example. Books from the TROG series, the MONSTER BOOKS, SPARKS (*Dinosaurs and Pink Pomegranates*) and the later BREAKTHROUGH books (*Mending a Puncture* and *The Paper Round*) offer interesting and possible reading material to all youngsters in the junior school, particularly those who are still at a very early stage of learning to read. Having books read aloud to them, either by their teacher or other children, will stimulate interest and

The teacher's role is to extend the children's interests to books they might otherwise miss, showing sensitivity to the needs of individuals and communicating her own personal enthusiasm.

make it possible for them to read in a context already known. This in turn will build up their expectation of enjoyment and success in reading and so generate further interest in books.

As children use the classroom collection teachers can make acute observations. They become aware of how books that have been read aloud are re-read. They can observe the way slower readers tackle books they know and have enjoyed, and how successful and persistent they are in having a go at reading them. Many teachers have noticed the way in which children can read beyond their supposed ability when the book is important to them for some reason, such as the enjoyment of the story, the appeal of its humour, or the particular information to be found. Often they turn again and again to a particular part to savour it anew, to share it with someone else.

Insights, gained as children are actively using books, give teachers the kind of knowledge that enables them to link their teaching to a child's present stage of learning and reading development. It enables them to guide children's reading throughout the primary school.

Extending language

Perhaps enjoyment of literature offers optimum opportunity for developing language, for within the 'world of the book' language is learned in a context of meaning and experience, where imagery and metaphor give life to words, as in the example given above from *The Boy who was Afraid*: 'the race formed by the ebbing tide', 'the small craft in its churn'.

Children can be helped to develop a sensitivity to language, a feeling for how the skilful use of words creates atmosphere:

> David stumbled, staggered, crawled: onwards in the darkness, uphill all the time: the going hard and stony: it must be a mountain slope ...
>
> *I am David*, Anne Holm (p. 22)

In the same story, David, who has known only the drabness of life in the concentration camp from which he has just escaped, awakens to a new world:

> ... a sea bluer than any sky he had seen ... near it lay villages whose bright colours gleamed dazzlingly ... and over it all shone the warming sun—not white-hot and spiteful and scorching as the sun had shone upon the camp in the summertime, but with a warm golden loveliness ... (p. 23)

For the first time David knows the true meaning of the word 'beauty'.

Children get hold of many words within stories. In Ulrich Thomas's *Apple-Mouse* they meet the word 'groom' as the bedraggled little mouse tidies himself up after the rain. The word 'unravel' occurs in Gene Zion's *No Roses for Harry*. In Rudyard Kipling's *How the Rhinoceros got his Skin* the word 'uninhabited' describes first the island itself and, later, the 'Altogether Uninhabited Interior'.

To be able to cope with 'book language' children simply must hear it often in stories read aloud to them. Margaret Clark makes this point well in *Young Fluent Readers*:

> Repetition of the same story read to a child has many values, not least the sensitizing of the child to the features of book language which is probably a far more valuable preparation for school than any attempts at teaching the child phonics or even a basic sight vocabulary.

The archaic language of fairy tales can only be met for the first time orally;

> There was a king of old who had twelve daughters. Some of them were fair as swans in spring, some dark as trees on a mountainside, and all were beautiful.
>
> Walter de la Mare, *The Dancing Princesses*

The solemn rhetoric of legend operates through the ear before the eye.

> The end of Nemerle's staff hovered silvery above Ged's breast. Once gently it touched him over the heart, once on the lips, while Nemerle whispered.
>
> Ursula le Guin, *A Wizard of Earthsea*

Children need the experience of listening to stories which begin with a description of the scenery, or the characters before the introduction of events.

> It was dusk—winter dusk. Snow lay white and shining over the pleated hills, and icicles hung from the forest trees.
>
> Joan Aiken, *The Wolves of Willoughby Chase*

If children are familiar with unusual names such as those of the Greek gods, they can take on otherwise quite simple retellings of the myths:

> Heracles was the son of Zeus, the Father of the gods, but he was born into the mortal family of Amphitryon, the Warrior Prince of Thebes.
>
> Ian Serraillier, *Heracles the Strong*

Without the experience of having such stories as these read aloud to them, even children who are quite competent readers will find them formidable and often incomprehensible. Gradually, we should help them to absorb the complex structures and styles that distinguish written from spoken language. They will learn about the conventions within narratives and gain the confidence to take on more elaborate stories for themselves. The language skills associated with listening, reading and writing, and discussion are all being fostered as teachers read aloud and share with children books that they too find pleasure and delight in.

Developing discrimination and personal taste

As children's experience of books grows, and they engage in discussion with each other, and with adults, so there is opportunity for them to develop taste and values, to become discriminating in their choice and appreciation of what they read. They begin to make judgments about the genuineness or artificiality of the situations or feelings in a book. They begin to notice how the author gets his effect, how the plot builds up, how the characters develop. They make comparisons with other books. They get to know particular authors.

Some of these points are apparent in the following excerpt from a recorded discussion of Clive King's *Stig of the Dump*. Six nine-year-olds, without a teacher present, are conjecturing about how Stig first arrived in the dump. Martin has put forward the idea that perhaps it was the result of a plane crash. They continue:

Martin: It might not even tell you in ...in the story itself. The story itself is really good

Children can be as much influenced by each other's taste as they are by the teacher's. Reading is a social as well as a private activity.

because some, usually stories start off like *The Hobbit*. Remember, it was all explaining, explaining who is who. Gandalf was this and Gandalf was that, but in this it goes straight on to what happened. Barney meets Stig and—

Mariangelo: But there could be another book showing this.

Almudena: Yes, like, the, could be—

José: Yes, like *The Witch and the Wardrobe* or something.

Mariangelo: Like *Five on a Treasure Island*.

José: It could be a continuation.

Almudena: Like Clifford. There's many books about Clifford.

Jane: Clifford just goes on and on. It doesn't say, hm, Clifford was a dog, and Margaret was a girl who owned a big, fat dog.

Marcelo: Yes, but—

Almudena: The, the, they might not know who we're talking about, Clifford is a dog. He's a great big red dog—

José: Yes, well, we're not discussing that. We're discussing about Stig and Barney aren't we? Now, Stig and Barney, here it says somewhere that, he lived, he had everything made out of old rubbish and things.

Apparent in this discussion is the children's understanding of the different ways in which stories can begin. They contrast a story that begins by describing the characters and what they do, and one that goes straight into the action. This is part of getting to know and be explicit about what one dislikes in books as well as what one likes, what one is prepared to put up with, perhaps, in order to get into a book. This is an essential part of developing personal taste.

Children need time to explore stories in their own way as in the above excerpt. Connie and Harold Rosen in their book *The Language of Primary School Children* make the point that 'one of the ways of talking about a story is to tell another one or one like it.' This enables children intuitively to pinpoint particular elements in stories which make them work, such as ways in which the plot builds up, and the use of suspense. Discussion with their teacher can help make them consciously aware of them.

Much of children's response to literature will be apparent in drama, art and music, and in both written and oral language, for literature unites affective and cognitive experiences and responses. We hear 'Who goes trip-trap over my bridge?' in children's play. We read 'once upon a time', 'with the gay young deer frisking in the forest', in their writing. The stories of the Trojan war may lead to a frieze depicting the opposing armies, the drama of Hector's death, or to the children's writing stories and poems about the heroes on either side.

It is important not to force response upon the children in any way that destroys the inner satisfactions to be gained from the stories. The most important response anyone can make to a story is talking about it, and for many children this means telling it. A general invitation to *talk* about favourite stories will stimulate a wide ranging discussion. General questions like 'What happens in stories?' and 'Can you visit the characters in these stories and what might they be doing now?' may serve the same purpose. The teacher plays a crucial part in developing discrimination, for it is she who makes opportunity for discussion, and encourages thoughtful, reasoned response, taking care not to induce the children to give her own responses, or to impose her own values.

Books become part of everyday living

However well-equipped and well-used the school library may be, it does not replace a good collection of books in a primary school classroom, for it is in the classroom that the teacher is aware of and in control of the total learning situation. It is there, too, that good stories are readily available, with immediate opportunity for talk and discussion. Children have the opportunity to establish which books are their favourites, which authors they like, which stories and poems they are fond of, and which picture books they want to pore over and delight in again and again.

The teacher, too, needs to know the books very well so that she can talk with children about their reading, draw their attention to other books, and guide them towards books they need and will enjoy. It is in this kind of 'cheek-by-jowl' situation that they come across books, that their friends call to them to share a particular something. They get to know and to seek out books liked and recommended by their peers. Thus books and reading become a natural part of classroom living and learning.

A classroom collection can truly be a most important aspect of a good learning situation, for it brings together teachers, children and books in a way that makes collaborative learning possible.

2

What Does The Collection Contain?

We have considered some of the ways in which teachers set up a classroom collection and so consciously contribute to literacy and learning. What we need to discuss now is which books to include and for what purposes. Only the teacher knows the children who are to use a particular selection: their special interests, their ethnic and social backgrounds, their past experiences and explorations. This knowledge is reflected in the choice of books.

The collection obviously includes fiction and non-fiction, though the distinction isn't always easy to make because story books often contain a mine of information and insights. The Bullock Committee found that narrative books were substantially outnumbered by non-fiction in many primary schools. It applauded the quality and range of information books that children 'dipped into', but deplored the fact that 'some capable readers almost never read a book in school'. It is necessary to keep the balance between fiction and non-fiction in mind. Perhaps a rule of thumb might be that there should be ten books per child in a classroom collection, to cover some of the needs for reading stories and getting information.

There is likely to be a core of permanent books such as an atlas, dictionaries, and books for identifying birds, flowers, and so on. Books will be displayed alongside classroom animals, current collections, or exhibitions. Others will reflect current interests, and may well be on loan from the school library collection. There will be attractive poetry anthologies and a good selection of picture books. At the core is the collection of fiction through which children meet all kinds of satisfying stories and through which they can enter the literary experience of the culture.

In this section we share our experience of the books that we see at the Centre for Language in Primary Education and that teachers have found useful in their work. For convenience we deal with them in recognised categories: picture books, fiction and non-fiction, poetry, books for urban children, particularly Londoners, and books that reflect the diverse interests of a multi-ethnic community.

PICTURE BOOKS

Children certainly enjoy and respond to picture books and soon develop their own favourites. Picture books offer to many children their first experiences of quality art. They provide special satisfactions in terms of visual stimulus and response to story and can play a significant part in developing children's verbal and visual imagination.

In their earliest book experience children enjoy nursery rhyme and ABC books illustrated by artists like Helen Oxenbury and Rodney Peppe. They enjoy the picture-story books of Pat Hutchins, such as *The Wind Blew* and the well-known *Rosie's Walk*; Helen Nicoll and Jan Pienkowski's bold-colour attractive books, for example, *Meg and Mog*; Brian Wildsmith's vivid jewel-like colour in books such as *Birds*, or *Squirrels*; and the real photographs in *Apple Mouse* by Ulrich Thomas.

Such books give children experience of many different kinds of illustration. Ezra Jack Keats in *A Letter to Amy* and Leo Lionni in *Frederick* use the medium of collage. In *Fish is Fish* Lionni uses soft crayons to portray underwater life and bright felt pens for above water contrast. Many of these media children use in school themselves for making their own pictures.

Wanda Gag's *Millions of Cats* is an example of a picture book in which the text and the illustrations flow together: the pictures of the gnomish old man wandering along winding roads followed by a growing procession of cats complement the refrain in the text: 'millions and billions and trillions of cats'. In this case, text and picture have been integrated so that the pictures do far more than simply decorate the text, or give a commentary on it, or extend it. The interaction of text and illustration is seen in Maurice Sendak's *Where the Wild Things Are.* For example, when Max is sent to bed his bedroom begins to change into a forest. The pictures gradually increase in size as his fantasy grows and his imaginary world takes shape. In Fiona French's *The Blue Bird,* beautiful pictures are in tones of blue, rather like a willow-pattern plate, until the Enchantress is defeated. Then the birds she has turned into stone become alive again and fly away, a many-coloured flock. The newly-won happiness shines forth in the brilliance of the pictures as the story reaches its conclusion.

Children enjoy humour, often richly shown in pictures as well as text. In John Burningham's *Mr Gumpy's Outing,* part of the enjoyment is watching the boat fill up until the inevitable happens and into the water they go. The animals dressed in the clothes blown from *Mrs Mopple's Washing Line,* by Anita Hewitt, are hilarious, but then pigs in pink petticoats are! No wonder Mr Mopple found it hard to believe Mrs Mopple's account of her day! Among the amusing pictures in *Animals Should Definitely Not Wear Clothing* by Ron and Judith Barrett is one showing a hen wearing stretch pants trying to lay an egg! Helen Oxenbury's *Pig Tale,* too, raises many chuckles as the newly-rich pigs spend their money on clothes and finally tear them off and dance a jig to celebrate their return to a pig-style existence. Raymond Briggs' *Father Christmas,* examining with disgust the 'horrible socks' given him as a present from Cousin Violet, is very funny. Richard Scarry's books, also in cartoon form but with busy dressed up animals, are pored over and enjoyed by very many children throughout the primary school.

Picture books appeal to all ages, including adults. It is a great loss to youngsters beyond the infant school when they feel themselves too grown up for picture books. Many folk tales are beautifully told and illustrated as single books—Carol Barker's *King Midas,* for example. *The Lion and the Rat* and *The North Wind and the Sun* are both traditional fables illustrated by Brian Wildsmith; *Amos and Boris* by

William Steig is a modern fable. *Why Mosquitoes Buzz in People's Ears* is a West African tale retold by Verna Aardema. Several of Rudyard Kipling's *Just-So Stories,* such as *How the Leopard Got his Spots,* are available in single editions and provide juniors with a rich experience of art and language. *When the Sky is Like Lace* by Elinor Horwitz, illustrated by Barbara Cooney, describes in words and pictures 'the splendid things that can happen on a bimulous night when the sky is like lace' and 'otters sing and trees dance, and the grass is like gooseberry jam'.

Through the Window by Charles Keeping is a deeply moving book with very complex pictures. On one side of a double spread, Jacob is shown peering out through lace-curtained windows, while on the other side the image is reversed and we look in at Jacob through the window from outside. Later in the book, after an old woman's dog has been killed in a street accident, there is a picture shivering with feeling which will move children as well as teaching them a great deal about human relationships. This is a powerful book that is likely to need adult mediation.

FICTION

One of our jobs is to help children to extend the range and quality of the stories that they are willing and able to cope with. We do this by reading and telling a wide range of stories to them and helping them to read them for themselves. For the youngest children we generally start from two directions: on the one hand, stories that clearly represent the familiar life experience of the child, and on the other, stories such as fairy tales that represent an alien (but symbolically familiar) environment.

Realistic fiction

Stories that set out to describe an environment in which ordinary children behave in ways that seem appropriate to them are a necessary component of any classroom collection. They reflect on and help children come to terms with the realities of living. Of course, aspects of the human condition may well be presented quite realistically in fantasy, but the term 'realistic fiction' designates especially those stories that could have happened to real people living in the familiar physical and social world. They concern people from a variety of cultural, racial, social and economic backgrounds, living in different times and places, and dealing with a range of human problems.

The strength of our collection of 'realistic' stories for very young children will come from such books as John Burningham's *The Blanket,* where the experience of losing and finding one's favourite bedtime talisman is sensitively described; Ezra Jack Keats' *The Snowy Day,* which tells of the city child's pleasure in discovering the possibilities of snow; Pat Hutchins' *Titch,* which shows the little boy always trying to keep up with his brothers and sisters; and Elizabeth Starr Hill's *Evan's Corner,* which describes the urgent need of a seven year old to find a corner of his own in which to keep his treasures.

Some of the graded reading schemes contain realistic stories that we might include in our collection for the younger age range: *A Rainy Day* (BREAKTHROUGH) is about the dreariness of arriving at school in wet clothes and having to stay in the classroom at playtime; *My Tooth* (LITTLE NIPPERS) describes a girl's delight when her tooth comes out in the classroom, the dismay and resulting chaos of dropping it and the triumphant relief of finding it in her shoe; *Lost at Football* (SPARKS) is about being taken by dad to a match during which little brother wanders off. Contrast these stories with the stultifying language, poverty of experience and total absence of feeling in some of the reading books given to beginning readers.

For the younger junior school child, the drama of living in an urban setting is less satisfactorily portrayed. There is Ezra Jack Keats' *Apt. 3* about an encounter with a blind man in a block of flats, which could lead to thoughts about how we come to understand our neighbours; Roy Brown's *Saturday in Pudney,* which is about children's group solidarities; and Bill Naughton's *The Goalkeeper's Revenge* which is a collection of short stories about a boy's growth in a northern

industrial town—invaluable for the teacher to read (selectively) aloud to the class. Philippa Pearce's *A Dog so Small* is a classic account of a boy's longing to have a pet in a London flat where it's not allowed and how he learns to adjust to the problem. John Rowe Townsend's *Gumble's Yard* and Mollie Hunter's *The Sound of Chariots* are both examples of gripping stories that have appeal for older juniors.

However, a familiar urban environment is only one factor in most junior children's reading. A historical setting can be an equally useful way of portraying the problems of growing up, as Hester Burton shows in *Otmoor for Ever!* Here, an eighteenth-century peasant boy feels humiliated at having to do such a girlish job as minding the geese, and gets in a fight with a gipsy boy who jeers at him; these are sentiments that any modern child can understand.

This incident raises the issue of sterotyped sex roles in children's literature. Educationists have become much more sensitive to the way in which little girls are invariably presented in subordinate domestic roles—playing with dolls and helping Mummy with the washing-up—while the boys go out and engage in adventures and responsible activities. And it is a sad fact that if we survey the works of even the best of modern children's authors we find a disproportionate number of male heroes.

In *The Children of the House* by Brian Fairfax-Lucy and Philippa Pearce, the eldest sister Laura explodes in anger at the Edwardian conventions that limit her sphere of action:

'I'm a girl. I'm older than Tom but it's Tom who will inherit Stanford. I'm cleverer than Hugh'—this had been agreed among them, without vanity on one side or rancour on the other—'but he's the one to be sent away to school, to be educated properly, so that in the end he can *do* something. I'm a girl; I stay at home; I wait to grow up and be married off.'

A similar fate is taken for granted in a large proportion of books about even modern girls. We shall therefore take care to supply at least some which offer girls a more positive image of their own potentialities. A few that spring to mind are: William Mayne's *No More School*, Noel Streatfeild's *Thursday's Child* and Nina Bawden's *Squib*.

We should add that some novels which have the deepest regard for naturalism as regards the emotional and social behaviour of the characters are actually set in wholly unrealistic historical circumstances. Joan Aiken's *The Wolves of Willoughby Chase,* and its sequels, rearranges English history so that steam railways, Stuart kings and packs of wolves roaming the countryside all coincide. Helen Cresswell, in *The Piemakers,* insists to the reader that her story of a pie made for the King to feed two thousand people is a true one. Of course, such a lack of circumstantial veracity is wholly unimportant so long as the system of sentiment and the behavioural patterns of the character match the child's knowledge of human nature.

Fantasy: animal stories

A diet of realism, however skilfully presented, cannot satisfy a child's appetite for novelty and extension of experience. One of the first ways in which children's stories diverge from normal life is in the introduction of talking animals and toys. Because children invariably talk to their pets and their toys as though they were real people, they accept unquestioningly that this should happen in books. The main advantage is that complex and emotionally charged experiences can be handled with less threat to the young reader than if the character were human.

The classic example of this sort of writing is in the Beatrix Potter stories. *Peter Rabbit* recalls the familiar experience of the child stepping outside the bounds of acceptable behaviour, finding himself in worse trouble than he had bargained for and thoroughly grateful to get back to the protection of his mother and good little sisters. *Tom Kitten* is about a child who cannot cope with the formal demands of respectable behaviour and dress—he doesn't *mean* to get into trouble but cannot help it. *Squirrel Nutkin* is about the awful child who bates the teacher beyond endurance while the other children watch breathlessly. Though set on a Westmorland farm three generations ago, these stories are as close to the real inner life experience of a modern child as any NIPPERS story.

We shall probably want to include in our classroom collection for infants some of the most popular 'talking animal' stories currently available in Picture Puffins—Jack

Kent's adaptation of the Danish Folk tale *The Fat Cat*, a cumulative story in which the gruesomeness of the events is overcome by humour and there are splendid repeat phrases for the children to join in, and Louise Fatio's *The Happy Lion* who, even at the end of the story, cannot understand why people are frightened by him. As in Pat Hutchins' *Rosie's Walk*, there is real satisfaction for the younger reader, for he knows what is happening better than the hero.

Talking animals extend into a wide range of stories, from Russell Hoban's *Frances* books which deal with the intimacies of family life, to Harwood Thompson's *The Witch's Cat* which is a highly original treatment of traditional characters. Robert O'Brien's *Mrs Frisby and the Rats of* NIMH, like Richard Adams' *Watership Down*, shows how the 'talking animal' genre can be used at a highly sophisticated level (for the most literate upper juniors) to explore serious themes about the search for a better form of social organization.

Fantasy: fairy stories and beyond

Traditional folk tales are an essential element in the classroom collection, to be enjoyed by all ages. (We should remember that originally they were 'adult' stories.) The most familiar of these come to us from three main sources: the French (collected by Perrault in the seventeenth century) which includes *Cinderella* and *Little Red Riding Hood*, and *Puss in Boots*; the German (collected by the Grimm brothers at the beginning of the nineteenth century) which includes *Hansel and Gretel* and *The Frog Prince*, and the English (collected by Joseph Jacobs about a hundred years ago) which includes *Jack and the Beanstalk* and *The Gingerbread Boy*. To these we can add the 'literary' fairy stories, such as Oscar Wilde's *The Happy Prince* and many of Hans Andersen's tales, which do not derive from the popular oral tradition but nevertheless retain the same characters and narrative conventions. The best version of Andersen's stories for reading aloud, and the only complete one, is Erik Haugaard's.

There are many reasons why we should pass on this great

European folklore tradition to our pupils. It represents the collective wisdom of our ancestors in the most satisfying of all narrative frameworks. The most common structure ('The Rule of Three'—the third son or daughter succeeds at the third attempt) is readily understood by the youngest children and is still enjoyed by older ones. The characters—princesses, woodcutters, giants and witches—are simple stereotypes whose moral qualities and behaviour conform to simple and predictable rules. The bad people (stepmothers, elder sisters, barons) are consistently bad, the good ones (youngest sons, poor widows, grandmothers) are consistently good. It is a satisfyingly simple view of life based on a moral system that Piaget refers to as 'transcendental'—having no regard for complex personal motives or shifts of attitude. Wolves and giants are there to be killed and it would be wholly inappropriate to see a situation from their point of view. On the other hand, the third son of a poor cobbler is worth a dozen lords and is fully entitled to the princess's hand in marriage.

These stories are available in a great variety of versions and editions, ranging from the LADYBIRD series which makes the characters in *Cinderella* look like Peter and Jane dressed up, to Philippa Pearce's sensitive adaptation of *Beauty and the Beast* in which the lucid prose, communicating a sense of longing and despair followed by tenderness and hope, is matched by the opaque mystery of Alan Barrett's beautiful illustrations.

Our selection of editions will depend on the age and sophistication of children. We need some general collections such as Raymond Briggs' splendid *The Fairy Tale Treasury* which has all the old favourites alongside some unfamiliar ones. The Hamish Hamilton collections of stories about *Princesses*, *Giants* and *Dragons*, concentrate mainly on modern 'literary' fairy tales with a strong appeal to the junior age range. Ruth Manning-Sanders' collections, such as *A Book of Princes and Princesses*, also greatly extend the range of stories that we can use with junior classes. We need to have the standard collections (Grimm, Andersen, Jacobs) always available in the most attractive editions. One very interesting thing to do is to read to children a variant of a familiar story; for example, we can read the Grimms' *Ashenputtel* and wait for it to dawn on the children that they're listening to another form of Cinderella; this can be followed by the English equivalent in Jacobs—*Tattercoats*. When they hear Jacobs' version of *The Three Bears* they will be surprised to find that the heroine is not Goldilocks but a little old woman.

We need to provide well-illustrated editions of single fairy stories so that a story can be savoured on its own. Additionally, it enables children of limited reading stamina to get through the whole book quickly, particularly if they have already heard it read aloud. In PICTURE PUFFINS we have Errol le Cain's exotic edition of *Cinderella* and William Stobbs' more down-to-earth illustrations to *The Little Red Riding Hood*, the latter in Perrault's original version where the story *ends* with the wolf gobbling her up. Another good paperback is Paul Galdone's *The Three Little Pigs* which has a most fearsome wolf.

We may want to have a few more luxurious hard back editions of single fairy stories, Oxford University Press does some beautiful editions of single tales illustrated by artists such as Brian Wildsmith, Bernadette Watts, Felix Hoffmann. Books like Paul Galdone's *The Three Billy Goats Gruff* are as delightful to look at as to read. Editions of this quality have the power to draw the most reluctant reader into browsing through them. For sophisticated top juniors there are more extended texts such as Kathleen Lines' retelling of *Dick Whittington* with illustrations by Edward Ardizzone and historical notes at the end. But we must beware the over-elaborate dressing-up of a story as much as the watering-down. The essence of the folk story is simplicity and directness of telling. It is a pity to choose versions that damage these qualities.

The fairy stories we have been discussing so far will be first encountered orally, the teacher telling or reading them to the whole class. Then children will enjoy rediscovering them in printed form. Only the more avid readers are likely to meet such stories for the first time in books. By then, they will have become so familiar with the conventions that reading them becomes extremely easy. Hans Andersen is the most advanced stage to be reached, for in his longer stories, such as *The Snow Queen* and *The Ice Maiden*, he devotes much of his time to description and explanation rather than to the concrete succession of events that characterises traditional tales.

From fairy stories, children will move on to heroic legend—tales of Theseus, Hercules, and, eventually, Beowulf. Simple episodic stories of national heroes successively destroying the enemies of society are readily understood by eight-to-ten-year-olds. These stereotype heroes have their modern counterparts in Superman, some war comics and the football stars. But whereas in the modern comics the heroes are delivering socks on the jaw and machine gun bursts to real human beings, in traditional saga it is symbolic figures of evil—trolls, Medusas, dragons—that are being fought. Versions of these stories need to be chosen carefully. The most acceptable translators now are Ian Serraillier, Roger Lancelyn Green, Barbara Leonie Picard and, for Beowulf, Rosemary Sutcliff. Most of their translations are available in paperback.

A special word needs to be said on behalf of Ted Hughes' *The Iron Man*, a modern myth about a small boy meeting the challenge of a great iron robot figure who in turn has to meet the challenge of a great monster from outer space; the power of the narrative and the simple but vigorous language is as impressive to a seven-year-old as to an adolescent; for many children the story is the most memorable in their early literary experience.

POETRY

From action rhymes to narrative verse

The smallest children enjoy playing with language, particularly when it is accompanied by physical movement. In the nursery and infants schools we play finger games and action rhymes that not only give the children enormous pleasure but also extend their knowledge of language and how it can be used. The two-year-old adores 'This Little Pig Went to Market' and 'Round and round the garden, went the Teddy Bear' because they combine exciting physical action with closeness to an adult. The essence of a dramatic story is being told in rhythmic language which is fun to repeat over and over again. By the age of four children are ready for more elaborate rhymes that can be played either with the fingers or with the whole body:

> Hickety tickety Rumpa rickety, Horny cup?
> How many fingers do I hold up?
>   ONE!
> You said one, we've just begun, a currant bun, shoot with a gun, look at the sun ...
>   TWO!
> One for me and one for you, one for my nose and one for my knee ...

(BREAKTHROUGH: Lollipops)

and:

> Little Robin Redbreast sat upon a rail;
> Niddle Naddle went his head
> Wiggle Waggle went his tail.

Teachers of small children will generally build up their private collection of favourite rhymes of this sort, often improvising and adapting them and discovering new ways of introducing them to their children. They become a shared and perpetuated oral tradition in the classroom and a natural part of the rhythm of school life. There are several published collections of action-rhymes suitable for this age range, of which the best and most easily obtainable is *This Little Puffin* by Elizabeth Matterson.

At the same time, the teacher will be introducing her class to the traditional nursery rhymes that she remembers from her childhood. Some of these have action accompaniment: 'London Bridge is Falling Down', 'Oranges and Lemons'. Others have elaborate narrative structures that require concentration: 'This is the House that Jack Built', 'Old

Mother Hubbard', 'Who Killed Cock Robin?' Most of them are for singing rather than for saying. But nursery rhymes also need to be said or chanted from time to time in order to focus attention more directly on to the words.

It is important that this pleasure of hearing, chanting, singing and acting verse should be maintained not just throughout the infants school but also throughout the junior school. Oral verse must form the basis of children's appreciation of rhythmic, patterned and poetic language. They can improvise or adapt new words to known tunes just as they can improvise tunes and percussion rhythms to accompany known words.

However, we will also be anxious to make written verse available to them. Their first introduction will be the recognition of nursery rhymes that they already know orally. Often, teachers have verse cards or home-made books of familiar rhymes available, perhaps beautifully illustrated with the children's own pictures. Others will have lying in the classrooms the twenty-four finely illustrated Nursery Rhyme cards that form part of the BREAKTHROUGH TO LITERACY series. Some of the BREAKTHROUGH story books also have nursery rhymes included at the end. There is a special pleasure in rediscovering a much loved rhyme on the page, particularly when it is well printed and illustrated.

There is of course an endless number of published collections of nursery rhymes which the teacher can have in the classroom for the children to browse through. Probably the most useful and relatively inexpensive anthology is Raymond Briggs' amusingly illustrated *The Mother Goose Treasury* which has over four hundred rhymes including all the best-known ones. The teacher's choice is likely to be governed by economics; the most beautiful are inevitably more costly. Brian Alderson's *Cakes and Custard* with pictures by Helen Oxenbury is in the luxury class, closely followed by Kathleen Lines' *Lavender's Blue* and Brian Wildsmith's *Mother Goose*, the latter containing better pictures but fewer rhymes. To add variety, teachers might like to include some inexpensive reprints of classic illustrated editions from the last century: Arthur Rackham's *Mother Goose*, Kate Greenaway's *Under the Window* and Walter Crane's *The Baby's Opera.*

Nicholas Tucker's *Mother Goose Lost* introduces a number of unfamiliar traditional rhymes, as do the Alderson and Lines collections. Unfamiliar rhymes such as 'Hickle them, Pickle them' and 'Alas, Alas for Miss Mackay!' enable children to enjoy robust humour and simple verse forms at an age when the well known nursery rhymes such as 'Baa, baa, black sheep' are being rejected as too babyish.

The stage beyond nursery rhymes is simple narrative verse, usually funny. The best recent example is Barbara Ireson's *One-eyed Jack and Other Rhymes.* A longer and marvellously illustrated verse story is Jonathan Coudrille's *Farmer Fisher,* a cumulative tale with delightful rhymes. And the Dr Seuss BEGINNER BOOKS are always immensely popular. *The Cat in the Hat* and *Green Eggs and Ham* have a vigour that compels the attention of children who might be reluctant to listen to conventional verse. A stage beyond this is nonsense verse: Lear's 'The Owl and the Pussycat' and Carroll's 'Father William' are the classic examples for younger children. There is a variety of good material from modern writers, ranging from T. S. Eliot's *Old Possum's Book of Practical Cats,* which is sophisticated humour that can be enjoyed by unsophisticated children, to Spike Milligan's *A Book of Milliganimals* and Charles Causley's *As I went Down Zig Zag.*

The Armada Lion Book of Young Verse, edited by Julia Watson, mixes pure nonsense of the Edward Lear variety with attractive trivia of this kind:

Algy met a bear
A bear met Algy
The bear was bulgy
The bulge was Algy.

The same crude wit, so well loved by small boys and at the same time giving a sly insight into human behaviour is shown in lines such as:

Auntie did you feel no pain
Falling down that willow tree?

Will you do it, please, again?
'Cos my friend here didn't see.

Nonsensical and humorous verse serves two particular
functions in the development of a child's experience. It
overcomes some of the fear that children and even some
teachers feel when confronted with the awesome edifice of
poetry, and it introduces children to a wide variety of
language patterns and structures that are immensely valuable, both when they attempt to write verse themselves and
when they undertake more serious poetry.

As children encounter more narrative poetry in the
classroom, they move from the level of 'Dr Foster went to
Gloucester' and A. A. Milne's 'Bad Sir Brian Botany' to
John Heath Stubbs' 'The History of the Flood', Robert
Browning's 'The Pied Piper of Hamelin' and the mediaeval
ballads. On the way they should have the chance to hear
and then read to themselves Ogden Nash's *The Animal Garden*
which is about a brother and sister who weren't allowed
animals at home but have the good fortune to be visited by
'shrivelled up, shrunken up Abidan Allseed' who creates a
magic garden full of unicorns, buffalo and kangaroos that
they can visit at night.

The satisfactions of narrative verse are similar to those of
any good prose story. When a good story is told in verse,
however, something is added to it. First of all, it is more
memorable; the form of the narrative is such that we can
recall and repeat it with satisfaction. Secondly, it achieves
greater vividness of detail and a more potent dramatic
impact:

Half-owre, half-owre to Aberdour,
'Tis fifty fathoms deep;
And there lies gude Sir Patrick Spens
Wi' the Scots lords at his feet.'

Descriptive and introspective poetry

It must not be thought that children's experience of poetry
should be limited to narrative, rhythmic or humorous verse.
Poetry which describes the private experience of the poet

and his observation of the world about him is a crucial part of their literary diet. Our starting point might be verse written by other children. *Junior Voices Book 1* contains a poem by an eight-year-old called 'Loneliness' which begins:

> Six boys teasing one.
> The one boy lonely,
> Cissy, cissy,
> It's not fair.
> The boy trying to ignore it.

The *Daily Mirror* competition-winning entries published in *Children as Writers* includes a poem by another eight-year-old called 'A Lament for a Dead Baby Bird' which commences like this:

> A baby bird is soft and cuddly, but when it dies it's lumpy and cold.
> If you hold it by it's leg it droops and hangs
> Dead as a doormat.

Verse of this sort, which is simple and unadorned with elaborate imagery but reflects an authentic emotionally-charged experience with complete accuracy, is exactly right for primary school children. They will examine the language, reflect on the truth of the experience, match it with what they have experienced themselves and (possibly) be inspired to write something like it for themselves.

Several adult poets have attempted to recreate the experience of childhood in their verse. The classic examples are Robert Louis Stevenson, Eleanor Farjeon, and A. A. Milne. Their most successful modern counterpart is Mike Rosen's *Mind Your Own Business*. He shares Milne's delight in skilful versifying:

> I've had this shirt
> that's covered in dirt
> for years and years and years.

and often uses traditional rhythms:

> This is the hand
> that touched the frost

that froze my tongue
and made it numb.

As a stimulus for children's own writing he is probably at his best in free verse:

I share my bedroom with my brother
and I don't like it.
His bed's by the window
under my map of England's railways
that has a hole in just above Leicester
where Tony Sanders, he says,
killed a Roman Centurion
with the Radio Times.

We will probably feel that this sort of verse satisfies and extends children's interest in poetry. We might then wish to push their experience on in two directions: linguistically, towards more complex and variegated imagery and verse forms, and, as regards content, towards sentiments and situations that are less familiar to most children.

The anthology which is most likely to guide and stimulate the child in both these directions is the four-volume anthology *Junior Voices* by Geoffrey Summerfield. This juxtaposes oral jingles, ballads and song texts with children's own writing, translations from foreign verse and the works of major American and English poets such as Theodore Roethke, Carl Sandburg and Robert Graves.

At first this collection might strike the teacher as well as the children as too bizarre and obscure for common enjoyment. But such an attitude is generally the result of an over-serious and intellectual approach to poetry—the sort of approach that consists of making sure one 'understands' it and can answer searching questions. Carl Sandburg's:

Why did the children
put beans in their ears
when the one thing we told the children
they must not do
was put beans in their ears?

is for reading for frivolous pleasure; once read and smiled over, it gets passed over for the next descriptive poem by Patricia Hubbell entitled 'Shadows' which demands a slightly more thoughtful consideration:

Chunks of night
Melt
In the morning sun
One lonely one
Grows legs
And follows me
To school.

The accompanying photograph makes the meaning of this poem clear. The complex metaphors are not there to be analysed, just felt.

The importance of *Junior Voices* is its demonstration that poetry for children need not be childish or coy. Nor, on the other hand, need it be archaic and Wordsworthian. It is simply language in use for powerful, evocative and often highly amusing purposes.

The problem of poetry in the classroom does not lie in the lack of good material, nor in the unwillingness of children ever to read it. The problem is how to present it in a relaxed, confident and pleasurable manner so that it is neither intellectually frightening nor emotionally sloppy.

NON-FICTION: CONTENT AND USE

If we want children to look upon books as a necessary and rewarding source of knowledge then we need plenty of non-fiction books in our classrooms, for two particular purposes. One is to support areas of learning which we, as teachers, are anxious for the children to study, such as the local environment, or the Norman Conquest. The other is to allow them to pursue their own particular interests and enthusiasms. If a full-scale project is planned, then the collection should include every possible book drawn from all available sources such as the school and local public libraries, and (for Londoners) the ILEA library at County

Hall. Additionally, we would ensure that basic reference books would be included, books such as *The Guinness Book of Records*, and a sampling of books relating to areas across the curriculum appropriate to children in the particular class.

Many teachers have a few relevant books in strategic places in the classroom. For example, if a collection of rocks and stones is of current interest, books such as *Collecting Rocks and Fossils* by J. B. Delair, *The Pebbles on the Beach* by C. Ellis, I. Podendorf's *Junior True Book of Rocks and Minerals* published by Muller, and Roma Gans's *The Wonder of Stones*, published by A. and C. Black have been used.

Curriculum books, for example in mathematics, might include counting books such as Tana Hoban's *Count and See*, and Helen Oxenbury's *Numbers of Things*; and Jan Pienkowski's *Shapes* and *Numbers* for younger children. Older children would have access to Isaac Asimov's *Galaxies* in the DOLPHIN SCIENCE series. Books such as Celia Berridge's *On my way to School* or P. Sauvain's *Along a Road* may both support or trigger off interest in children's immediate environment. David Macaulay's beautiful books, *Cathedral: The story of its construction* and *City: A story of Roman planning and construction* shows the creation of a cathedral in the former and a city in the latter, from their conception and at various stages during their construction. Macaulay's fine pen and ink drawings give the reader some idea of what it is like to be a builder perched high on a scaffold, as well as the names and purposes of such things as flying buttresses. *How a House Happens* by Jan Adkins shows through clear text and diagrams, including blueprints, the steps that go into building a house.

Children are generally interested in animals and often keep them in school. Niko Tinbergen's *Animal Behaviour* and *Tracks* by E. A. R. Ennion and Tinbergen, could find a place in any primary classroom. For junior children, books about ants and spiders, such as Ralph Whitlock's *Spiders*, are valuable adjuncts to learning.

Children's personal interests should be reflected in the collection. For example, the LADYBIRD *The Motor Car* and *The Motor Car* (Macdonald Junior Reference Library) are often favourites. *Coin Collecting: A Beginner's Guide* by R. F. Johnson and books about fishing, horses, puppets and ballet, enable particular youngsters to read about their present experiences and understandings and to take their interests further.

When a child is genuinely seeking answers to real problems, then notions of 'age-level' and 'readability' in books suddenly appear strangely irrelevant; adult books are often more helpful and 'easier' than children's books, and less able readers find themselves using materials that would normally be regarded as beyond them; *The AA Book of the Car* is a good example. On the other hand some picture books which are often used with younger children have such detailed and authentic pictures that they too can provide a rich source of information. *The Web in the Grass* by Berniece Freschet, with illustrations by Roger Duvoisin, is one such book.

Changes in the classroom collection, as books are returned to the central library and new ones take their place, reflect the changing and growing interests of the children. A range of books is required because information books, picture books and stories, old and current newspapers and periodicals and old documents can all become resources for learning. How children use a range of resources is illustrated in the following account of third -and fourth-year juniors. These children see things in the classroom animal collection, or at the museum, or on the sea-side holiday and naturally turn to books to classify, corroborate, analyse and interpret.

Interpretative comments are interwoven with Mrs Judy Hargreaves' account of how she and her class integrate experience and books into truly collaborative learning.

FROG AND TOAD ARE FRIENDS

Two boys, inseparable friends, had found what was thought to be a toad under a log. Using the *Clue Book of Freshwater Animals* they set up a terrarium to keep it in. One of them could struggle through the instructions with support; the other one was basically a non-reader. Neither knew the word 'turf,' but others had seen it somewhere. It was the 'Turf Accountant' in Roehampton!

The complicated connections were slowly worked out, and at the same time a collection of books to go with the toad was set up, using the school and the public library. Paul basically learnt to read by using *What I Like about Toads* (Judy Hawes). I had read this to a group; other interested children had read it to the toad boys. Both read *Frog and Toad are Friends* (Lobel) and the sequel with great pleasure. In spite of the relative simplicity of the text, the content—including the humour—was highly relevant and appropriate.

When children raise their own questions they search a range of books for information. They often find that, instead of answers, a new set of questions is sparked off and the search continues. (Compare the ongoing inquiry of these children with the textbook type of question where the answer is to be found within the text.) They become critical readers as they begin to realise that some books do the job better than others, that some books actually contradict each other

During their hours of observation and investigation and simple recording one of the problems which came up was the leaping ability of toads. They had found that theirs could leap forty-seven centimetres. In the Wheaton book one of the main ways of differentiating frog from toad was the much greater leap of frogs. Was forty-seven centimetres a long leap or a short leap? If it was a short leap, how ever far did frogs leap? With the help of a very fluent reader gradually all the books were consulted and one had a paragraph discussing 'the powerful back legs of a toad enabling it to propel itself forward with its characteristic long leaps'.

Everyone involved had come to realise that books are not always correct or accurate. This whole problem had provoked critical reading. Perhaps this emphasizes the need to provide more than one source of reference and to provide different kinds of books using many criteria to select them. Besides, there was much to recommend the book published by Wheaton: for example, the page on the enemies of the toad and the frog which was also the idea central to the storybook *The Old Bullfrog* by Berniece Freschet.

The teacher has selected the books with care to cover the immediate interest as well as the long-term curriculum:

> In the toad collection I had deliberately excluded the MacDonald STARTER on the subject. There was, however, a MacDonald STARTER in the room on *Spiders*, and one of the toad enthusiasts while browsing through it was impressed to discover that spiders are capable of 'playing dead', a feature in common with toads. Now, books on spiders and ants are a part of the permanent class collection as they seem to crop up so regularly. On this basis I took Ralph Whitlock's *Spiders* out of the library. The children were thrilled by the illustrations. Some of them read it from cover to cover, excited by the statistics: e.g. 'the weight of insects eaten by spiders in the world each year is more than the weight of all the people living'.

The children make connections between their own experience and book information, and then they find themselves using books for their own purposes which cut right across artificial categories of 'information', 'reference', 'non-fiction' and 'story' books.

> I took my class on a series of outings to the Thames at Putney, Hammersmith and Barnes and asked for an ILEA library loan—books like Eric de Maré's *London's River* were included in the set sent. I was disappointed to find that it was of little use to these particular children. I knew what I would encourage the children to pay attention to, but each trip was full of surprises, and it was interesting to look at some of the connections the children made.
>
> The highlight of one trip was the clear foot prints made by three different kinds of birds, leading to the use of the *Clue Book of Birds, Pond and River Birds* (J. Leigh-Penberton), LADYBIRD, Collins' *Bird Book*, and *Swan Upping* by J. Palmer. The *AA Book of Birds* was a particular favourite with the children. The pictures of birds are very

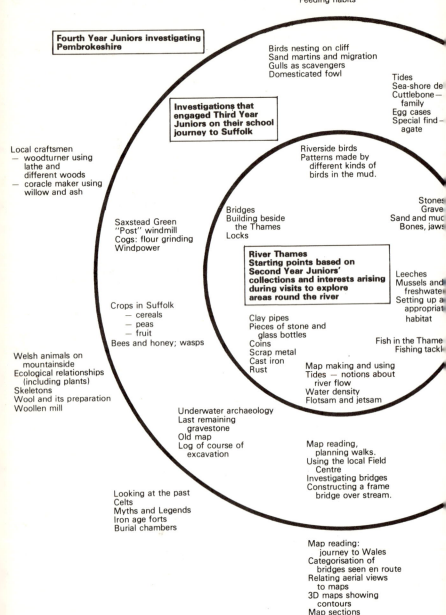

Bird families
Identifying and
    respecting birds'
    eggs
Bird pellets
Colonies of birds
Feeding habits

Fourth Year Juniors investigating Pembrokeshire

Birds nesting on cliff
Sand martins and migration
Gulls as scavengers
Domesticated fowl

Tides
Sea-shore de
Cuttlebone —
    family
Egg cases
Special find —
    agate

Investigations that engaged Third Year Juniors on their school journey to Suffolk

Local craftsmen
— woodturner using
    lathe and
    different woods
— coracle maker using
    willow and ash

Riverside birds
Patterns made by
    different kinds of
    birds in the mud.

Saxstead Green
"Post" windmill
Cogs: flour grinding
Windpower

Bridges
Building beside
    the Thames
Locks

Stones
Grave
Sand and muc
Bones, jaws

**River Thames
Starting points based on Second Year Juniors' collections and interests arising during visits to explore areas round the river**

Leeches
Mussels and
    freshwate
Setting up a
    appropriat
    habitat

Crops in Suffolk
    — cereals
    — peas
    — fruit
Bees and honey; wasps

Clay pipes
Pieces of stone and
    glass bottles
Coins
Scrap metal
Cast iron
Rust

Fish in the Thame
Fishing tackl

Welsh animals on
    mountainside
Ecological relationships
    (including plants)
Skeletons
Wool and its preparation
Woollen mill

Map making and using
Tides — notions about
    river flow
Water density
Flotsam and jetsam

Underwater archaeology
Last remaining
    gravestone
Old map
Log of course of
    excavation

Map reading,
    planning walks.
Using the local Field
    Centre
Investigating bridges
Constructing a frame
    bridge over stream.

Looking at the past
Celts
Myths and Legends
Iron age forts
Burial chambers

Map reading:
    journey to Wales
Categorisation of
    bridges seen en route
Relating aerial views
    to maps
3D maps showing
    contours
Map sections

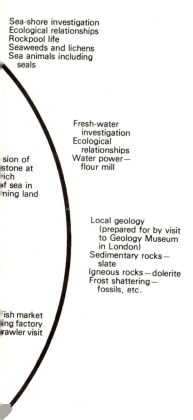

Sea-shore investigation
Ecological relationships
Rockpool life
Seaweeds and lichens
Sea animals including
  seals

Fresh-water
  investigation
Ecological
  relationships
Water power—
  flour mill

sion of
stone at
ich
f sea in
ning land

Local geology
  (prepared for by visit
  to Geology Museum
  in London)
Sedimentary rocks—
  slate
Igneous rocks—dolerite
Frost shattering—
  fossils, etc.

ish market
ing factory
rawler visit

The chart shows some of the areas reported by Judy Hargreaves,
investigated by her pupils over a period of three years. It is interesting to
see how the collections and interests encountered in explorations of local
environment are starting points for enquiry over several years, in
different environments, and could well continue beyond school.

clear, authentic information is presented in a straightforward way, the lay-out of the book and the index helped
the children identify what they were looking for. Details
given, such as the types of bills, varieties of nests, raised
many questions. One small group pursued this bird topic
only, and on each return looked for more clues. Someone
else found small lead weights and rebuilt a fishing line by
looking at various books on fishing methods.

Many people made simple stone collections and
browsed through a book of Henry Moore's sculpture—so
did the bone collectors—going on to read *The Wonder of
Stones* (R. Gans), *Secrets in Stones* (R. Wyler and G. Ames),
and a geology museum publication on *Rocks and Minerals*.
A child with a piece of pumice, having established that it
originally came from a volcano, asked for a story book
with volcanoes. I was puzzled: it turned out that she
meant Fiona French's *Blue Bird*; 'picture books', which are
so often regarded as suitable only for infants, still have a
big role for older children. Peter Spier's and Richard
Scarry's pictures are an unexpected source of valid
information as well as being enjoyable things to look at.

Clay pipes were found and the only relevant book
turned out to be Peter Spier's *London Bridge is Falling
Down*: 'Give him a pipe to smoke all night ... suppose the
pipe should fall and break'. The discussion of the
marvellous details in this picture gave a group a
remarkably authentic base of enquiry as to who smoked,
where the tobacco came from, and the historical period.

Old newspapers, including *Daily Graphics* for 1899 were
both fascinating—particularly the adverts for pop in glass
marble bottles—and very valuable. They were used to
provide authentic background for plays the children were
writing that took place in 1899.

The incident which I found the most exciting was when
Genevieve insisted on collecting and bringing back river
water to school. She had a very clear supposition. She
wanted to compare equal volumes of river and tap water

for their weight, and she was extremely satisfied with the result: tap water was heavier. As a result of our river visits she had read the water sequence in Richard Scarry's *What do People do All Day?*, in which water purification is shown to include the addition of alum, soda, and lime.

She was convinced that they must still weigh something even if you couldn't see them.

In fact, Richard Scarry's water sequence became an excellent reference for the whole notion of the start of a river and its journey to the sea, culminating in 'See you later, water vapour!' This, in conjunction with E. and G. Rose's *The Big River*, the children's comments and questions, made me realise what very complicated notions are involved. Maps helped some children, too. Some of their understanding of rivers was to understand Tien Pao's predicaments in *The House of Sixty Fathers* (DeJong).

By the time I took my group on school journey, we had a vast shared experience of stories, prose, poetry, and reference books. It would be impossible to comment on all the significant connections which I noticed and these in turn were probably only the tip of each personal iceberg of the interchange between literature and experience. To give some idea, I will take a few things from a day at Dunwich on the Suffolk coast.

This coast is being steadily eroded by the North Sea. Once, it is recorded in the Domesday Book, a wealthy town of fifteen churches, represented by two seats in Parliament, existed; now, it is a small village with the last gravestone of the last churchyard within a metre of the cliff's edge. The cliffs are sandstone, pitted with sand martins' nests.

When we arrived at the cliff-edge, *The Iron Man* was instantly recalled. Another child, watching the soaring seagulls, was reminded of a favourite passage from *His First Flight* by Liam O'Flaherty in Barry Maybury's *Wordscapes*. This tells of a young seagull unable to take the plunge and learn to fly like his brothers and sisters.

Famished and teased by the prospect of food, he eventually stumbles and flies. Several weeks after first hearing this passage, Ruth learnt to swim and explained to me that it was like a seagull learning to fly. Her description was fabulous, using many parallels with the ideas of the passage and also taking on the style as she told of being suddenly able to swim. On the cliffs at Dunwich she searched for likely ledges for seagulls. She told us too, about how the sea was inviting—she could swim—she would be able to do it. She reminded children and adults of the analogies she had made eighteen months earlier with *His First Flight.*

Underlying many parts of the school journey there seemed to be a personal challenge to their ability to cope with each new situation. *I am David* was constantly referred to amongst the children themselves and this was further reflected in the poems, music, and stories written after the journey.

On the cliffs we looked at the gravestone and later the local guidebook gave facts about the rate of erosion. In the back of it was a log of the divers who are making archeological investigations of the ruins on the sea-bed. This made good reading in a style which some children had not met.

On the beach we found what turned out to be a rare agate, identified for us by the Geology Museum. It had been brought down from a Scottish volcano in the ice of the glacial period.

In the course of this experience, all kinds of books are totally integrated into the learning environment of the classroom and are referred to automatically when particular questions arise. Children engaged in learning in this way are becoming *autonomous learners,* able to extend their knowledge and interest at will, without always having to refer to an adult.

But, though the children appear to be in control of their own learning much of the time, a lot of work has had to be done by the teacher. In particular, over a period of time, she has taught her children how and why to use books as they were actually using them. She has chosen and obtained many of the books that are being used. This has involved care and knowledge. In addition to using the school library, she regularly browses in book shops and in the Centre for Language in Primary Education library. She makes use of the facilities offered by the local authority's library for the long term loan of books, and for borrowing particular collections of books (e.g. the river collection she describes). In addition, she visits the local library where she is allowed to borrow up to forty books at a time. The children are allowed up to four books each on their fortnightly visits. This not only adds up to a fair number but enables changing and developing interests to be catered for as they arise.

The children themselves bring in contributions in the way of books, pamphlets, maps, photographs and so on. As in most classes, there are 'experts' on such things as birds, cars, football and the Second World War. Books written by these 'experts' become available for general use.

Getting to know books as she and the children use them has enabled this teacher to develop various criteria that help her to make her selection:

—the overall appearance of the book should attract a child to pick it up and browse.
—information books should be accurate and up-to-date. A five-year-old book on Africa, for example, is often out of date.
—people and places should be presented as they are, not as stereotypes (Eskimos living in igloos, Brazilians cele-brating carnival).
—matters of fact should be clearly distinguished from opinions. For example, in books about dinosaurs, facts related to their size and form, and the geological periods when they were alive need to be distinguished from theories about how they became extinct.
—illustrations and diagrams should be clear and effective guides to understanding the subject.

—the information should be readily accessible to the reader by means of a clear table of contents, good design and layout, an appropriate index, relevant and understandable illustrations and diagrams, an annotated bibliography.

The classroom teacher knows that one doesn't need to read a book right through to make good use of it; and that we do not always use books for the reasons that the author might have intended—as when we use a volume of Breughel pictures for information about sixteenth-century costume. Above all, she judges the books by the use that children can make of them, as they seek to find answers to worthwhile questions and extend their pleasure in the pursuit of knowledge.

Reading materials that belong to everyday life

If reading is for, not apart from, life, then the materials in the classroom should include a variety of texts which are part of the children's world and readily available in their own locality. This ranges from magazines and weeklies such as *Woman's Own*, the Sunday colour supplements, *Radio* and *TV Times*, and the local newspaper, to the football rule book and programmes, travel documents, *Dandy* and *Beano*, music and 'pop star' magazines, DIY manuals, printed advertisements from various sources and recipes and patterns. By including these in a classroom collection one acknowledges the validity of what is read outside school and has a common basis for sharing the children's experience. The major contributors to such a selection will be the members of the class, so it will be constantly changing and reflecting their current interests. It is perhaps unnecessary to add that there might be only one feature or article from a particular magazine which will be appropriate, and such cuttings can be assembled into a scrapbook, or mounted for wall display.

Books made by children

Additionally, children's own writing produced as books should take its place in the collection. Making such books can be an exciting and important venture involving both teacher and child. In creating a book for a wider audience the child gets real experience of authorship. He creates a world in which he is in control and in doing this he is exploring his own world on his own terms, and inviting his readers to consider his point of view, his notion of a good story. Making a book to be shared in this way brings together many different aspects of learning. For teacher and child, it encompasses a study of the diverse ways in which we use spoken and written language.

PARTICULAR NEEDS AND INTERESTS

Urban life

There are more substantial, less ephemeral 'reads', written *by* as well as *about* a local community. These can be found in the kind of selection Centerprise offers which includes books like *Hackney Half-term Adventure* by Ken Worpole and John Boler, Lil Smith's *The Good Old Bad Old Days*, and the poems of Vivian Usherwood. Several series such as SPARKS, COLOUR KNIGHTS, STEPPING STONES, NIPPERS and BREAKTHROUGH show modern urban children of many cultures at play with their peers in the local streets and parks. However, series are often not of a uniform standard—for example, the controversial NIPPERS. While *Knitting* is genuine and funny, other books seem to verge on caricaturing working people and lack authenticity.

There is a range of books relating to London children which represent the immediate and familiar as well as the distant and the exotic. John Burningham's *Humbert* is a delightful book for youngsters who may well have seen the Lord Mayor's show. Charles Keeping's *Wasteground Circus* tells the story of two boys' engagement with a travelling circus doing a one-night stand on the demolition site where they play. Also by Keeping, *Richard* (a book about a police horse) gives inside information about horses in London. Keeping is, very consciously, a Londoner. His *Charley, Charlotte and the Golden Canary* will evoke responses from many children who have seen their old homes demolished and replaced by high-rise flats with the accompanying disruption of family and friends. *Runaway Danny* by Celia Berridge tells about Danny, also changing homes, hopeful of moving to the country. He is disappointed to find himself living in a high-rise block. Berridge's illustrations give a remarkable child's eye view of urban roof-tops as Danny gazes from his window and sees trees and grass in the distance. He misses his old friends and doesn't find it easy to find new ones, so he runs away to the 'country' which turns out to be Greenwich Park.

For older children, *Smith,* by Leon Garfield, is set in bygone London. It's a sophisticated book, well worth a teacher's time spent in sharing and discussing it. In *London Bridge is Falling Down,* with its intricate and detailed drawings of nineteenth-century London, Peter Spier offers a mine of information to youngsters interested in the past. Carol Tate's *Rhymes and Ballads of London* is full of chants, rhymes and jingles, while the Opies' *The Lore and Language of Schoolchildren* offers a challenge to children and teacher alike to make their own collection of local songs and chants and share in the fascination of noting the variations in words and tunes. Three recently published books, *Say Goodbye, You May Never See Them Again* by John Allin and Arnold Wesker; *Rabbit and Pork—Rhyming Talk* by J. Lawrence and *Cockney Ding-Dong* by Charles Keeping, may well become classics of London literature.

A multi-ethnic community

Just as local life-styles must be recognised and valued within a school, so too must cultures and beliefs from further afield, and overseas. Many classrooms are representative of different cultures, among them, Hong Kong, the Caribbean, West African, the Punjab, and Cyprus. If books are to represent the real world for all these children then they must show children as they are. This is as important for white children as for black children, for Asian as for African children, for English as for West Indian children.

Additionally, all children benefit from gaining understanding of other points of view, of other cultures. The classroom collection will include folk tales and everyday-life stories from other cultures.

The Children's Book Trust, New Delhi, has just such a selection representing the tradition, past and present, of a part of the Asian sub-continent. In Margaret Kidd's *Ashok's Kite*, the people are clearly Indian, but kite-flying is enjoyed in city parks as well as rural Asia. Ezra Jack Keats writes about youngsters who happen to be black in an American inner-city setting. Peter's attempts to whistle and his antics in the city are familiar experiences, so *Whistle for Willie* is about the feelings of children experiencing life not just of an ethnic minority. Stories that consider the feelings of people, as well as giving a true background are important. Reba Mirsky's *Thirty-one Brothers and Sisters* does this in an authentic representation of life in the Kraal. Older youngsters will enjoy *The Leopard* by Cecil Bodker, about the adventures of Tibeso, a young Ethiopian boy, who was the only one who knew that the local blacksmith, not a leopard, was stealing the cattle. The blacksmith catches him and leaves him in wild country at the mercy of the beasts. There is some poetic justice when the blacksmith is himself killed by a leopard.

Myths and folk-tales are one way of sharing and comparing the differences and similarities of a variety of cultural traditions, and the Anansi stories. Both West African and West Indian versions, are an obvious example. The 'tricksie' Spider Man is to be found in the folk-lore of many countries. Even more universal is the use of guile by the less exalted to humble and outwit the more powerful. In *A Story, A Story*, Gail Haley presents a thoroughly Ghanaian story, with the English text conveying the rhythms and repetitions of Ashanti. For example:

> It is raining, raining, raining.
> Should you not fly into my calabash
> so that the rain will not tatter your wings?

The illustrations are full of African patterns familiar to those who have seen the richly patterned cloth worn by many West Africans. Comparing this with the many Caribbean versions of Anansi is just one way of showing how folk tales change as each culture makes them its own. Yet another interesting comparison can be made between Anansi and the Monkey King, that cunning hero, so admired by Chinese children. R. Bertol's *Sundiata,* the epic of the lion king, is a legend from Mali in the oral tradition, showing Islamic beliefs and a great and subtle wisdom, which older children will enjoy. Another interesting aspect of the multi-ethnic approach can be found in *Folk Tales from Asia for Children Everywhere,* UNESCO-sponsored books, containing folk tales from countries such as Bangladesh and Vietnam.

Whereas easy-to-read books provide an easy read for a child, books of real quality should be the first choice for reading aloud. These can then be made available to the children to try to read for themselves as well as simpler versions. It is in books of high linguistic quality that a real sense of story is conveyed.

Having elaborated in some detail the value and richness of Anansi stories, it is salutary to remember that Caribbean cultures do not rest solely in folk tales, even though they are an important strand. There need to be books about social organisation, history and adpated life styles. Karl Craig in *Emanuel goes to Market* gives a lively account of a Jamaican market and the mishaps brought about by the unexpected intrusion of Lico the parrot. Markets the world over have a fascination and appeal as well as giving the atmosphere of a particular area or country.

More books of a multi-ethnic character set in England are now being published. For younger children there are such books as *Bubu's Street* by Beryl Gilroy set in an area of decaying old houses and new tower blocks; *My Brother Sean* by Petronella Breinburg is about beginning school; another book is about playing at doctors. *Sean's Red Bike* is a third book by the same author. Older children will like *Another Home, Another Country* by Mary Cockett, which deals with some of the problems that arise in adjusting to a new way of life. Again, it is the intrinsic quality of the book which is of prime concern. The use of stereotypes, of just presenting visually a 'statutory' black, does not make a book good. Here it is interesting to compare *Things We Like* (LADYBIRD KEY WORDS 3A) with *The Bike* (BREAKTHROUGH) or *Knock at Mrs Herbs* (NIPPERS).

THE BRICK STREET BOYS is a series of amusing picture books with many ingredients to appeal to urban children. Young juniors would enjoy the cartoon humour of these books. Unfortunately, *Here are the Brick Street Boys* disqualifies itself by the final page which is a most offensive stereotype picture of six caricature African cannibals boiling white children in a cauldron. This points up the danger of relying upon a series *in toto*.

There is a range of good stories such as *Janey* by C. Zolotow, *Carrie's War* by Nina Bawden, *Dorp Dead* by Julia Cunningham, which centre on themes such as loneliness, prejudice, self-knowledge and identity, experiences which are common to all children in differing degrees and which can be discussed together. A good realistic book brings out many facets of controversial issues such as colour, sex and prejudice because the authors are considering the clash of human values.

Finally, there is no case to be made for making a category of literature that is exclusive to any particular ethnic or socio-economic group. All children need to respond to stories that tap the roots of childhood itself. They share a range of emotional response. They know what it is to be lonely, or afraid, and of the struggles to find and maintain oneself within a family, or amongst peers. They experience the powerful human emotions, love, joy, hate, jealousy and loyalty. They all need to see themselves reflected in some of the stories they read in the books around them, taking part in their everyday world. Books about schools, supermarkets and so on need to show people going about their ordinary lives, for all children are curious about their world and want to know about it and be part of it.

3
Organising and Using the Collection

In the Bullock Report the statement is made,

> There is no doubt at all in our minds that one of the most important tasks facing the teacher ... is to increase the amount and range of [their] voluntary reading (p. 126).

We are all aware that teachers' influence on the books children choose is considerable, particularly for children for whom reading is not a normal part of their everyday lives. It hardly needs saying that the choice of books available determines what is read. Good book selection, a basic source of teacher influence, is obviously an important factor in the whole business of reading. A teacher reported recently that when she took her class to the public library she, too, chose a book which she read in the classroom at a time when the children were reading their books. She found that on their next visit to the library some of the children had taken note of the book she had been reading and were looking for books by the same author.

In order to make a good job of selecting books teachers need to know books as well as know their children; it is not enough to know the readability level of the book and the reading age of the child. The important questions are: what will make him laugh or feel sad? What will excite? What will give him the opportunity to reflect, to identify, to deepen his understanding of self, to begin to understand others and the way they behave? In other words, will this book get to him?

Many of us can remember periods of obsession with such books as Richmal Crompton's *William* series; stories of school life as in books about Jennings; and now we see children 'eat up' Enid Blyton. We can take children further by opening up new horizons. In the case of the books of Enid Blyton, in which gang psychology plays an important part, this means introducing them to other books in which groups of children work together towards a common goal, such as Erich Kästner's *Emil and the Detectives* or Roy Brown's *Saturday in Pudney,* or in which there is treasure or reward to be sought and found, as in E. Nesbit's *The Story of the Treasure Seekers* or Tolkien's *The Hobbit.* In this way, we use our experience and knowledge of children's literature to bring to their attention significant books that they might otherwise miss. Books appeal to children at different times in their lives. Books such as Pat Hutchins' and John Burningham's picture books are most enjoyed in the nursery and infants' school. In common with books such as the Dr Seuss books, they can provide rich and satisfying experiences with literature, and perhaps make learning to read more worthwhile.

Of course books can be enjoyed at various levels even if they are not immediately understood. Pat Hutchins' *Clocks and More Clocks* is a case in point. It is a great moment for a child when he suddenly realises why Mr Higgins has a problem!

Obviously class teachers will want to take part in choosing the books. Many teachers invite their children to take part, too, not only in selecting from the school's central collection but also by encouraging them to check with their local children's librarian, and by occasionally taking them to the nearest good bookshop where as well as browsing they can come back with a few self-chosen paperbacks.

Many fine children's books are available in paperback. However, even with a very tight budget, it is important that the collection contains some books that are beautiful in themselves. Of course, personal taste is a determining factor here, but books such as Randell Jarrell's translation of *Snow-White and the Seven Dwarfs,* illustrated by Nancy Burkett, is certainly worth considering. *And Miss Carter wore Pink* by Helen Bradley, set in Edwardian England, is another. *The Bayeux Tapestry* by Charles Gibbs-Smith is a worthwhile buy for any primary school.

THE INFLUENCE OF THE LOCAL LIBRARY

In the previous chapter (page 49 et seq.), Judy Hargreaves refers to the constant use she and her class made of the local library, and the part it played in catering for their changing and developing interests. Many schools have a close liaison with the local librarian and they work together to build children's awareness of what the library offers and how it can be used.

In Margaret Clark's recent study (*Young Fluent Readers*) of thirty two Scottish children who learned to read before entering school, she comments on 'the extent to which the local library was a regular and valuable source of reading material' for these pre-school readers. She comments on the important role of the library 'in catering for and stimulating the interests of these children'. 'For most of them the stimulus to use the library came initially from the parents, though it was clear that the children themselves later found it a valuable source of information and enjoyment.'

Margaret Clark draws attention to the fact that in the public library young children are often allowed a freer choice from a wider range of books than is permitted in some classrooms; she says:

> The role of the class and school library and the development of greater links between school and local library in order to provide wide enough resources is certainly an aspect worthy of further consideration. Just as some local libraries had regulations sufficiently flexible to enable them to cater for the interests of children such as these, so also some schools see their class libraries, their school libraries and the local library as all part of an integrated service catering for children's needs.

> ... We do perhaps tend to underestimate the potential of many children or stay too close within an age-related structure in considering their likely interests. This seems particularly true with boys, judging by the evidence of the interests of a number of the boys in this research (p. 103).

Knowing the local library influences not only children's

choice of books but that of teachers, too. It is another source for seeing and getting to know books. It is a good way, in this era of paper-backs, of ensuring that a few of the more expensive hard-backs find their way into the classroom collection.

ADMINISTERING THE BOOKS IN THE SCHOOL

Books find their way into the children's hands from a variety of sources: the classroom collection, the school library, the Local Education Authority library, the local public library,

The central collection of books at this primary school is housed in the corridor outside the classrooms. Children use it freely throughout the day.

Non-fiction books are arranged in a simplified Dewey Decimal Classification (see page 88). New or specially interesting books are displayed prominently. The collection includes books written and bound by children. A large proportion of the fiction is kept inside each classroom. Teachers and children regularly select collections of books to meet current learning needs. Children, with their teacher's consent, are allowed to take any books home.

Teachers take it in turn to be responsible for ordering books. Accessing, shelf maintenance, etc., are done by an ancillary helper.

not to mention the occasions when teachers and children bring in their own books to share with each other. Somehow these books need to be organised to meet the immediate needs of the children so that there is always *maximum accessibility.* We have to ensure that children can put their hand to the right book as soon as it is needed. In some schools there is an emphasis on classroom collections, while others emphasise the central school library. How the two should relate to each other is the subject of the following discussion between Judy Hargreaves, a class teacher, and Griselda Barton, formerly Library Organiser for ILEA.

G.B.   The way that I see it: the classroom collection is there for the immediate use of those children with that teacher. It's a very personal situation. But the school collection should be servicing it so that when the classroom interests change, the resources change to suit what's going on. We should have a school collection which is (*a*) servicing the class-room collection and (*b*) holding the things that can't be included in the classroom collection, like large reference books and certain expensive items which you can't afford to have in every class-room. But the whole thing should be completely inter-connected and it's just a matter of where you locate certain things to make them available.

J.H.   There should be certain good quality books in the classroom that would be there because of their intrinsic value. I feel that there is a very strong need to have good books in the classroom all the time.

G.B.   A danger is that the classroom collection might become totally static.

J.H.   The initiative comes from the teacher *and* the children.

G.B.   This is ideal, but it goes wrong for all sorts of organisational things: the attitude of the head, for example. The acquisition of books may be seen in purely administrative terms, rather than from a learning and teaching point of view.

J.H. And also the philosophy of the school which may differentiate books according to children's age.

G.B. Ideally, impetus comes from the classroom. People responsible should be organising in the light of the needs that have been expressed by the people who are actually going to use the books. Panic buying happens when the person with responsibility is given no time—if she's simply told, 'here's a sum of money' without time to consult colleagues.

J.B. The teacher responsible may be in the position of having to foist books on some members of staff. Even when they're taken on she has no way of knowing how they're used.

G.B. You need somebody, preferably full-time, at least with sufficient time, who is, well-informed and who orders, buys, catalogues, updates what is in the classroom. For example, checking ISBN numbers can take hours. Then you've got somebody who understands what is going on in the school so that she knows what is likely to be relevant. What is crucial to successful connection between collections is a clear understanding of what is going on. These are some of the jobs to be done by the teacher with this responsibility:

First, knowing what's available and communicating this to colleagues.

Second, routine getting of books and organising them.

Third, maintaining a proper *flow* of books geared to the needs of particular classes.

The responsible teacher's job is made possible if the school has an agreed book policy, including a purchasing policy. It is essential, too, that all the staff know what is available and how the system operates for locating what they need quickly.

Many schools adopt positive strategies to make sure that teachers, and often children, too, have the opportunity to see new books as they arrive. Sometimes, groups of books are put in the staffroom for a week and discussed informally and at a staff meeting. In another school the entrance is used for displaying books and time is allocated so that children and their teachers can browse among the new books, and try earmarking some of them! In another school teachers are regularly invited to bring along to staff meetings a favourite book and share it with their colleagues. In this way teachers who may not have had the opportunity to get to know children's books are introduced to a range of books and may well become really enthusiastic about them. All of this tends to increase the amount and range of voluntary reading in the school. Edward Blishen talking of the effect of a teacher's enthusiasm on children said, 'As teachers we can do neither more nor less than present to our children a spectacle of reading *in action.*'

Calling attention to books

Neither teachers nor children will get to know books readily if they are shut in cupboards or stored higglety-pigglety in classroom shelves. Nursery and infant school children need to have most of their books displayed in a way that allows the whole cover and title to be seen. In one old infant school, shelves have been built along one side of a wide corridor. Books are displayed enticingly along the shelves, a long, bright strip of carpet has been acquired, and small comfortable easy chairs placed in strategic spots. This is in addition to classroom collections and an attractively-arranged disused cloakroom that houses the central collection.

Books play a vital part in many schools, accompanying displays, supporting particular themes or celebrating special occasions. Attention is drawn to them at assemblies, or when children share their work with children from other classes, or with their parents.

PROBLEMS OF GRADING AND COLOUR CODING BOOKS

As far as 'information' books are concerned, it is probably impossible to devise any system for grading books according to 'difficulty'. Nor are we likely to want to do so, since the reader adopts his own strategies in seeking information for them; he can *use* and *enjoy* them without being able to read all the text. One comes across virtual non-readers poring over a copy of the Reader's Digest *Book of British Birds,* or Richard Scarry's *Great Big Air Book,* and learning a great deal as they do so.

However, many schools do find it helpful to separate out the fiction into categories according to reading difficulty. This is to enable the child to go straight to a group of books that he can feel confident about coping with, so that he won't have to sort through a lot of difficult books that will only frustrate him. The teacher will also be able to limit her search for books for a particular child by turning to the most appropriate section. Most classes are likely to have children with a spread of reading ability of at least six years and some organisation of material must be thought out.

The problems of grading books are, of course, enormous. There are no standardised formulae that will quantify the comparative 'difficulty' of, say, Eric Carle's *The Very Hungry Caterpillar* (only 18 sentences long, an interest level of four to six years, a lot of repetition, lavish illustrations and a text whose 'readability level' is 10) and Alan Garner's *The Owl Service* (173 pages, no illustrations, a very obscure theme, but also a measured 'readability level' of less than 10).

A completely effective grading system would have to consider not just vocabulary and sentence structure but *overall length* (children's stamina varies according to the reading experience and their enthusiasm for a particular story), *familiarity with the story* (a story already known is read with greater ease than a totally new one), *narrative structure*

(Leon Garfield's *Devil in the Fog* opens with the highly emotional outpourings of the first person narrator which present quite different problems for the reader from the book that begins with reported dialogue), *illustrations and layout* (every phrase in Stan and Jan Berenstain's *Bears in the Night* is placed beside the corresponding section of the picture so that the meaning is made doubly clear).

More important even than these formal characteristics of the book are the intellectual and experiential demands being made on the reader. Polly Donnison's *William the Dragon* requires the reader to know how eggs normally turn into chickens and David McKee's *Six Men,* though superficially very simple, involves the reader in complex notions of group organisation, justice and mixed motive. This leaves one with the realization that a text may be easy for one child but difficult for another of apparently equal reading abil- ity—because every reader brings a different range of knowledge to the task.

Teachers might well decide, in the face of such a complex range of issues, that they can do no more than rely on plain common sense and intuition. But this common sense and intuition must be based on, first, a thorough personal knowledge of each book and, second, an intimate knowledge of the children who are going to read it. If it is considered helpful to do a standardised 'readability test' such as the Fry (guidance on this is available at the Centre for Language in Primary Education), then it must be recognised that these only measure the ratio of syllables to word and sentence length and ignore all the crucial factors discussed so far in this section.

A final problem must be faced. If we separate the books into bands, then we have to make sure that a child doesn't feel *obliged* to confine his choice to a particular level. Children (like adults) want sometimes to enjoy the satisfac- tion of an 'easy read' and some of the most enjoyable material for able readers might often be found in the lower bands of the collection. In other words, banding must be seen as an indication of the reading difficulty, but not as a strait- jacket on reading choice.

OWNING YOUR OWN BOOKS

There's a special pleasure to be gained in actually owning your books. Since quality book shops are not always very close to schools, many schools operate clubs and bookshops in order to enable and encourage children to build up their own bookshelves.

Help in organising and stocking your own shop is available from the School Bookshop Association (see page oo). It is a very straightforward operation and the benefits to the children are immeasurable.

Kate Austen, head of an infants school, writes here about how such a bookshop operates in her school, and the way the children respond to the opportunity of owning their books.

INFANT SCHOOL BOOKSHOP
Open every Wednesday afternoon, 3.00–4.00 pm, in the School Hall

We are all aware of children who are able to read but who do not read, partly because their readers in school may be dull and unimaginative, and partly because the reading material available to them outside the school is limited. Because of this, and also because we wanted to encourage children to buy books of their own choice, we decided to open a little school bookshop to which parents and children might come.

We approached this venture rather tentatively, for our school is in as disadvantaged an area as any other. Nevertheless this factor only encouraged us to persevere. We advertised our bookshop by posters made by the children, and letters were circulated to our parents inviting them to come along and see.

Kathie Halpenny (Teacher with Scale post for Library) stocks the shop with beautiful inexpensive paperbacks at 20p–30p each, though we do have some more expensive books costing 50p, and Ailee Currie (Teacher with Scale post for Home/School) stands behind the counter discussing the books with the children and parents,

The school bookshop at work—it is open every Wednesday at the end of school so that as parents come to collect their children they can spend time together browsing, and perhaps buying a paperback to add to the child's private collection.

while Sheila Webb (our fantastic secretary) sets all the books out, labels them, and handles all the accounts. All the other members of staff bring their classes along, some to buy, some just to look — and as parents come to collect their children the sales begin.

We all think that our bookshop seems to have affected our children's general attitude to reading in the school and all our staff have noticed a much keener appreciation of books generally, and classroom book corners as well as the school library are all more eagerly frequented.

Kirstyn — *6¾*   When asked why she wanted to own books and buy books Kirstyn said, 'You grow up with them, and then you think Oh; I've had this book for a long time, and you love it because the story and pictures are so lovely.'

Brian — *6¾*   Brian explained, 'You can read your own book any time you like. I like *Frog and Toad* books and so does my Mum.'

Megan — *6*   Megan said, 'I love them when they are all shiny and new, and I read them myself and Mummy can read them to me. I like looking at the pictures, and you don't have to do what Mummy and Dad says about Library books, 'cos these books are your very own and you can do what you want with them.'

Sometimes children review books they have read and liked and we read the reviews out at Assembly and display them by the bookshop. Here is a review by Chima of *Pirates* a book in the FIRST FACTS series edited by Brenda Thompson.

Pirates
This book is about Pirates who sail in their ship, and fly the flag of the skull and cross-bones called the Jolly Roger. They capture a treasure ship and fire their cannons and escape with the treasure and put it in a deep hole on a secret island. Another ship, a war-ship captures them and takes them back to England. I think a boy would like this book. A boy of 6 years. It cost 25 pence. There are lovely ship pictures. *Chima*

USING BOOKS IN THE CLASSROOM

In this section two teachers share with us ways in which books are used to promote learning. In the first example, Jane Herbert writes about the enjoyment infants' school children get from books and ways in which their responses can be seen.

ENJOYMENT FROM BOOKS

The book areas are now such an integral part of the
classroom environment that it is difficult to remember
what things were like when all we had in our rooms was a
basic reading scheme plus a few supplementary readers.
True, there was a library from which teachers could take
a story for the end of the day and which also had a rather
dull collection of information books. Now every room has
its own library with a large and varied range of books.

Many of the children's favourite stories have common
elements, books with giants, dragons, monsters and
witches, some of whom are friendly and un-threatening.
Tomi Ungerer's *Zeralda's Ogre; Lyle, Lyle, Crocodile* by
Bernard Waber; Louise Fatio's *The Happy Lion*; and
Frank Herrmann's *The Giant Alexander* are examples of
stories that our children enjoy.

There are stories with situations and feelings with
which a child can identify. Often the hero is small, but
somehow, he wins in the end. Pat Hutchins' *Titch* and
Brian Wildsmith's *The Little Wood Duck*, Peter Nickl's *Ra
Ta Ta Tam* about a small man who manages to build a
small engine, and *The Giant's Feast* by Max Bolliger, are
examples of this kind.

Of course as we built these up we worried that many
books would be spoilt, lost, or stolen, but these fears have
proved unfounded. We still have a school library from
which extra books can be selected so that special interests
of an individual or a group can be pursued in greater
depth, but in each class there is a core of books that reflect
the particular personality and interests of that group of
children and teachers. In this situation it is natural for
children to feel that books are a part of their environment. They make some porridge, the story of the Three
Bears is at hand; they look at the fish, there is a book full
of information and pictures to be shared with a teacher,
as excited by the contents as the child. A book about
Roman cities — *City* by David Macaulay — is taken

into the corner at story time; John Burningham's *Mr Gumpy's Outing* is shared by a small group of children, remembering the story, picking out some repetitive phrase, talking about the pictures. A child who has shown her teacher a loose tooth is listening to her read *The Loose Tooth* (BREAKTHROUGH). Later she will read the book on her own, or perhaps share it with another child or teacher. In this way it can be seen that books and reading link in naturally to much that the children are doing in and out of school.

Through having large and varied book areas in each room we are now beginning to learn far more about our children's response to books, which books they like and how they use them. There are books which have an immediate appeal, like many of the Seuss books where there is a humour in the illustration and play with words, or where, as in the Berenstains's *The Bike Lesson* or *Bear Scouts* the action is built up from page to page with father bear always in trouble, and the small bears always right.

Zion's *Harry the Dirty Dog* is another popular book. The funny situation can be seen from the pictures as well as easily understood from the text. Pienkowski's *Meg and Mog* books have a great appeal, and children love to share them together. The stories have great humour and are easy to remember and the print is an integral part of the pictures which makes them ideal early reading books. Carle's *The Very Hungry Caterpillar* with its attractive layout is another well-loved book often shared between children. The children like looking at many of the information books, especially some of the Macdonald BEGINNERS' WORLD and STARTERS.

But we found it is not enough just to put books into the library areas and expect children to make wide choices. Often it is only after finding a book through an adult that they will return to it themselves. We found this with Maurice Sendak's *Where the Wild Things Are;* contrary to expectation it was not a book children chose for

themselves, but after it had been read to them several
times and talked about, they returned to it themselves.
The John Burningham little books, *The Snow, The Blanket,
The Friend* and *The Baby* are books that children can soon
learn to read after sharing them with a teacher. They
identify with the books, the home is real, the drawing
detailed and there is a complete event, a simple story, in
each book. Other books that they can relate to are the
LITTLE NIPPER books and some of the BREAKTHROUGH
series. There are books where the illustrations are pleasing
but difficult to understand, e.g. *The Hippo who wanted to Fly*
by Robin and Inge Hyman. One child chose the book and
talked about the pictures for several days before listening
to the story.

Information books are in constant use, and we all feel
that our interests and horizons have been broadened, as
adults and children have been able to find things out
together, and to share knowledge that is new to both of
them. We no longer feel that we should know all the
answers to the questions; indeed, we think it important
that the children should see that there is much we do not
know, but that the desire to find out and that books are a
rich source of information is what is important. Amongst
the many books we use we find the TRUE LIFE and some of
the Macdonald series particularly valuable, but we have
many other information books, suitable for a wider range,
including adults.

Not only have we become more aware of the children's
direct response to books; we are beginning to see how
much books are able to influence and enrich their school
experiences. We see evidence of the children's response in
the language they use, their imaginative play, their
drawing and painting and the stories they write. Andrew
and Michael have just brought a painting to me; it has a
castle, and knights riding, and the language they use
shows the influence of books: 'The knights have to learn
how to ride a horse', and 'they are practising sword
fencing, — that man doesn't want to be a knight. There is

a well, in those old-fashioned days they didn't have taps, the string is wound round the handle, and they have to wind the bucket up. There are two doors to go in, but Andrew forgot to do the drawbridge, — the water was to keep guard of the castle so nobody can get in, unless the drawbridge is down — they fall in the moat, scrunch, splash.' No one had prompted Andrew and Michael to go and paint this picture and the language came from their pleasure in a story, *The Little Knight.*

We saw an example of imaginative play in the child working with bricks who had built himself a cave 'because I'm a dragon, with big wings so I can fly, and there's fire coming out of my nose'.

Another child did a collage of a witch on a broomstick, and talked about the witch's house he passes on his way to school, with 'two black cats and a broomstick outside it'.

Many of the children's drawings and paintings show the influence of stories, especially the traditional fairy and folk stories. Looking round the school there are paintings and drawings of Cinderella, Jack and the Beanstalk, the Princess and the Frog, the Three Little Pigs, a magician in his study, a dragon, and many witches.

The children's writing shows the influence of stories, ranging from the simple, 'Once upon a time Cinderella went to the ball', to the more complex where there is a blending of known stories, the children's own experience, and sometimes their fears and worries.

I think it is clear that for us the classroom libraries are an integral part of our school. It is through their constant use that the child is himself drawn to reading. It is as he uses books that he can learn to understand them, to absorb the language to be found in them, and thus learn to read with enjoyment and understanding.

In this second example, Ken Mines, a class teacher at Princess May Junior School in Hackney, describes his work on environmental studies, using a considerably wider range of reading materials than is usual with young children.

OUR LOCAL ENVIRONMENT

The teacher doing environmental studies may work from either the particular or the general environment, using a wide variety of source materials. By 'particular', I mean the neighbourhood local to the school — the child's own streets; 'general' refers to the kind of study undertaken through the use of printed textbooks, TV, and so forth. Both types have their merits, but for various reasons the 'particular' approach has been more successful with both teachers and children of Princess May Primary School, in Hackney. Here I shall outline a study carried out by a class of eleven-year-old children of average or above-average ability, and follow this by another study made by a class of seven-year-olds of below average ability. Both classes contained a very high proportion of West Indian, Greek and Turkish children. I shall draw attention to the source-materials we used (these sources, including book titles, are italicised).

Looking through the *school's old records* (Log Books, Admissions Registers, etc.) we noticed that the names of pupils 20 or 30 years ago were very different from those of the present day. This started a discussion about names, and why some were more popular than others. We thought it might be interesting to take a sample of forenames from the 1940s and 1970s and plot the results on a histogram. We found that while the present generation sported several Tinas, Traceys, Lindas, Learies and Leons, with Arnette, Sonul, Delle, Mehment, Kemi, Melanie, and a host of others making single entries, in 1940 Harold, William and Herbert for the boys, and Ivy, Louise, Gladys, Alice and Lily for the girls were in a slight lead. Very few names appeared on both histograms, and, notably, on the later graph no name appeared to be a clear favourite.

The children soon worked out some of the implications

of these differences, in terms of altered population and the whim of fashion. The next question was, 'How can we find out about names from earlier times?'

The school records did not go back beyond the early years of the twentieth century, so we discussed other sources. At last somebody said, 'What about the weddings book?' So we made a visit to the local church vestry and asked if we might look at the *church records*. A sympathetic rector opened a safe, and produced a register of burials dating back to 1559. The children seemed impressed by its age, and the clarity of the writing. With a little help they succeeded in compiling two lists, men and women, and two more histograms were produced.

The differences were very noticeable; Elizabeth and Anne, John, William, Thomas and Richard, were all clear favourites. Many of the men's names were common and still in use (Peter, Roger, Bernard, Andrew), but fewer women's names had continued to be popular. Several were completely obsolete — Pallas, Hippolite, Foulke. Can *you* guess which sex applies here?

Our blood was up, and from the church registers similar samples were taken every hundred years in the intervening period. The graphs showed that forenames remained remarkably consistent during this period, few 'novelties' appeared, and the same ones were always top: John, William, Thomas and Richard; Elizabeth, Anne, Mary. The project could have ended here, but with a *churchyard* stuffed with old graves it seemed a pity not to go and look at them. These we found dated from the eighteenth and nineteenth century, and we were able to make rubbings or take photographs of several. Back in school we could examine at our leisure not only names, but also various attractive letter styles and materials suitable for display. (The lettering, together with the burial registers already consulted, was an added bonus and provided material for an entirely different project.) Many of the graves were illegible. To the question, 'How

can we find out what was written on them?' the almost
stock answer came, 'The Library'. There, indeed, we
found that an industrious Edwardian had copied all the
inscriptions; they were bound up in a *manuscript book,* so
here was an introduction to yet another book of source
material.

But, how to match grave and inscription? We asked,
and were shown a *plan* of the churchyard with an *index* to
the names: therefore, having a name, we could find the
grave, and vice versa. We were moving from maths to
detective work!

One girl had spotted an unusual surname —
'Peppercorn' — while she had been working with an
eighteenth century burial register; in the graveyard we found
two graves bearing this name. Could we find out anything
about them?

In fact, we already had some information. Earlier the
class had looked at Stoke Newington Church Street, the
original village site. A standard reference book in most
libraries is *Kelly's Directory.* This lists, by trade and by
street, alphabetically, London's shops and commercial
premises. By consulting first the directory for 1976 and
then an earlier edition (1878), we had been able to
compare present-day shops with 100 years ago. Among
these was a Thomas Peppercorn, Grocer and Tea Dealer.
Obviously we remembered so apt a name, but more
important, we knew his address. Since these directories
are published annually, and in one form or another date
back to the 1850s, it is possible to discover how long any
shopkeeper remained in business, what he sold, and if the
shop still exists.

This had taken us away from the original survey of
forenames, but we hadn't quite finished. We knew the
most common names for Stoke Newington; what about
the rest of the country? Back to the Library we went,
where we found *The Guinness Book of Names* by Leslie
Dunkling, Chapter 5, 'Fashionable Names', told us where

first names came from, that 'Tracey' was first given by Jean Simmons in 1956 after Spencer Tracey, and the way in which social class influenced the popularity of some names. For our purposes, the section of the most popular names was most useful, although it only went back to 1838 — not nearly enough. Imagine our surprise to find that for boys' names *our* first four were not only the same as the National Survey (taken in England and Wales), but in the same order of preference. Here was (I suspect) an instance of 'discovery method' where the teacher was more surprised than the pupils.

Here the survey ended, but it was clear that more could have been done, and from time to time the children or I found additional material suggesting further research: *Gravestone Designs* by Emily Wasserman, *Discovering Epitaphs* by G. N. Wright, and *Graveyard Wit* by P. Haining, as well as plays and stories about people buried in the local churchyard. Several books on heraldry were useful for information about one or two 'top people' whose graves were found locally. Interest was aroused in styles and calligraphy (the eighteenth-century long *s*, *i* for *j* in Benjamin (sixteenth century), and old spellings. Apart from the church registers we found *Printed Epherema* by J. Lewis and *The Penguin Book of Scripts* by Fairbank useful.

You will notice that none of my sources is fictional and they are all 'adult' references. Usually the children preferred these to the few 'junior' versions, and with a little help sorting out the more difficult sections they presented few problems. The lack of fiction was regretted, but nothing worth while turned up in this study, although *Oliver Twist*, which the children knew, and *Sketches by Boz*, which they didn't both provided a wealth of authentic and often unusual names. It was noticeable after the study how sensitive the children had become to the names of people, and several brought in library books to show me the names in the story. As I have said above, these children were of average or above-average ability; less able, or younger, children would obviously need different material and a different approach, although clearly some aspects of the survey (looking at old church registers, rubbing graves) would not have been too difficult. In contrast, however, I conclude with a brief reference to a study made by a class of below-average seven-year-olds.

In this case the project was 'The School'. Again the school's Log Book was used. This was started in 1901 by the splendidly named headmaster, H. Wakerell. (Log books, if not in the school, might be in *County Hall Archives* — teachers could check this for themselves.) At the time we had been unable to find any *old photographs* of the school, although subsequently these did appear, one from the *Photographic Unit of the GLC* at The County Hall. We also found out something of the history of the school from the *Greater London Record Office,* and the *Map and Print Department,* which sells photocopies of old maps, both at *The County Hall.* In addition, the teacher consulted *Schools* by D. Smith and D. Newton, and *Learning and Teaching in Victorian Times* by P. F. Speed in the THEN AND THERE series, from Longmans. Other books which later became available were *Edwardian Album* by N. E. Bentley, and John Betjeman's *Victorian and Edwardian London from Old Photographs.*

Since reading these references was beyond the children's capabilities, the teacher provided stimulus-material from them, and read extracts from the log-book. They learned about the 'Standards' ('Standard 1 Geography. Plan of School. What a map or plan is. Idea of scale.'), 'Drill', a school closure in 1902 for 'Coronation Holidays', and absences due to a cart-horse parade. The children wrote, drew or painted, and produced a model of the school.

Since we did this project, a further source has appeared. An advertisement in the *local paper* produced several replies from *old pupils,* and the loan of *old photographs.* One ex-pupil has made several visits to our school, and has become very friendly with the children, on one occasion producing several prizes for 'effort'. She has given an interview full of fascinating detail: the step-up 'platforms' in the classrooms, open fires, frequent use of the cane, Empire Day celebrations, 'American tea-parties'. Another correspondent actually remembers Mr. Wakerell's retirement ('We gave him a tool kit because he intended building his own car').

The above is a very sketchy and inadequate account of environmental studies in operation. In particular, it misses much of the excitement of original research which is shared by pupil and teacher alike; also the wide range of activities possible. I have not said much about maps, photographs (the children are now developing their own pictures in the school's newly-installed dark-room), nor the wealth of material to be found in the streets (lamp-posts, letter-boxes, bollards, coal-covers, iron railings and balconies, decorative roof-tiles, cast-iron 'Gothic' capitals on bay windows and so on).

What I hope is clear, is that when doing environmental studies, almost anything can be useful, and this includes dipping into books written for a more 'general' approach. Among those which we have at present in our classroom collection are: PEOPLE OF THE PAST series, FOCUS ON HISTORY series, DISCOVERING YOUR ENVIRONMENT series, *The Great Fire of London* by E. Stones, the DISCOVERY series by P. Sauvain, STUDY BOOKS and E. Hunter's *The Story of Arms and Armour*. Some of these are more useful than others and, as a rule, take second place to the type of material I have mentioned earlier.

What Ken Mines and Jane Herbert have achieved, in their different ways, is the personal involvement of their pupils with books so that the children learn that books are a necessary and personally rewarding part of life.

4
Sources of Information About Books

With so many new children's books being published each year, it is not easy to keep up to date with them. This section lists a variety of sources of information: book lists (pages 84–6), books about children's books (pages 86–8), books about organising the book collection (pages 88–9), and bookshops and book clubs (pages 89–91).

BOOK LISTS

Books for Children: The Homelands of Immigrants in England JANET HILL (Institute of Race Relations, 1971) SBN 85001 012 8.
The content is dated, but this book remains a helpful guide to the problem of selecting material for immigrant children.

Books for the Multi-racial Classroom JUDITH ELKIN (Library Association, Youth Libraries Group, 2nd edition, 1976) SBN 85365 069 1

Carry on Reading JO KEMP and JANET FARRELL (National Book League, 1975) SBN 85353 217 6
A list of books, both fiction and non-fiction, which have been found popular with children who have just learned to read but who are still 'diffident'.

Children's Books of the Year ELAINE MOSS (Hamish Hamilton, in association with the National Book League and the British Council, published annually since 1971)
An annotated list, both fiction and non-fiction, arranged in sections for easy reference, of the best books published during the years from 1970 onwards. The annotations are some of the most helpful to be found anywhere.

Children's Stories: Fiction, Verse and Picture Books for the Primary and Middle School BERNA CLARK (School Library Association, 1974) SBN 900641 20 7
Over 500 entries, ranging from picture books for the youngest

children up to stories and poems for ages 11–12. Paperback editions are especially noted.

The Cool Web: The Patterns of Children's Reading MARGARET MEEK, AIDAN WARLOW and GRISELDA BARTON (Bodley Head, 1977) SBN 0370 10863 9
A collection of papers by scholars and authors ranging from W. H. Auden and Beatrix Potter to Professor D. W. Harding and the neuropsychologist R. L. Gregory. Between them they build up a rationale for story-making and for literature as essential components of a child's education.

Each According to his Ability: An Annotated List of Books and Other Materials for use by and with Mentally Handicapped Children MARGARET MARSHALL (School Library Association, 1975) SBN 900641 26 6
A list of items, including charts and kits as well as books, for children who are mentally handicapped because of various forms of disability.

English for Immigrant Children JUNE DERRICK (National Book League, 1973) 85353 174 9. [Revised edition in preparation, under the title *English as a Second Language.*]
Books, both fact and fiction, visual aids and other materials, for use with children of all ages and by teachers.

Fantasy Books for Children NAOMI LEWIS (National Book League, 2nd edition, 1977) SBN 85353 260 5
A copiously annotated, wide-ranging list with a short introduction that has important things to say about fantasy books.

Fiction, Verse and Legend: a Guide to the Selection of Imaginative Literature for the Middle and Secondary School Years DOROTHEA WARREN and GRISELDA BARTON (School Library Association, 1973) SBN 900641 15 0 [Updated edition in preparation.]
This list is aimed at older children, and the books are grouped under various headings. There is a bibliography of books and periodicals about children's books.

Looking at London: Books and Other Media for the Primary and Middle School (School Library Association, 1974) SBN 900641 22 3 [Supplement in preparation.]
A list of items — books pictures, slide sets, films and music — compiled by the London Branch of the SLA and fully annotated.

Myths, Legends and Lore RALPH LAVENDER (Blackwell 1975) SBN
631 95230 6
A list of books for children, with filmstrips and records of
language and music in another section.

Paperbacks for Nursery Schools SHELAGH WEBB (National Book
League, 1975) SBN 85353 226 5.

Poetry for Children DENYS THOMPSON (National Book League, 1973)
SBN 85353 163 3

Read and Find Out: Information Books 6–9 BARBARA SHER-
RARD-SMITH (National Book League, 1975) SBN 85353 228 1
A list of information books for children from 6–9 years, to open
new horizons and satisfy new interests — but especially to enjoy.

Read and Find Out: Information Books 9–13 BARBARA SHER-
RARD-SMITH (National Book League, 1976, sequel to above)
SBN 85353 241 9

Reading for Enjoyment, 2 to 5 year olds ELAINE MOSS SBN 85504 008 4;
6 to 8 year olds JOAN and ALAN TUCKER SBN 85504 009 2; *8 to 11
year olds* JANET HILL SBN 85504 010 6; *11 year olds and up* AIDAN
CHAMBERS SBN 85504 011 4 (All edited by NANCY CHAMBERS for
Children's Book Centre, 1977) [From National Book League.]

World in Stories: Books for Young People selected for Geographical Interest
JUNE and JOHN ADCOCK (School Library Association, 1972) SBN
900641 13 4
The 200 books in this list are mostly stories; many are suitable for
primary school children, and they are grouped by continent and
indexed by country.

BOOKS ABOUT BOOKS AND CHILDREN

Children and Fiction E. W. HILDICK (Evans, 1970) SBN 237 35186 2
Contains some important insights into the relation between
reading and literature.

Children and Stories ANTHONY JONES and JUNE BUTTREY (Basil
Blackwell, 1970) SBN 631 12590 6
There are strong points about the importance of stories in
children's lives, what response to expect, and what criteria to use.

Children are People JANET HILL (Hamish Hamilton, 1973) SBN 241
02243 6

Written by a children's librarian working in the community, the book contains significant thoughts about the interaction between people and books, and how this can be brought about. A very personal view.

Intent upon Reading MARGERY FISHER (Hodder & Stoughton, 2nd edition, 1964) SBN 340 03510 2
Subtitled 'a critical appraisal of modern fiction for children', the author discusses different kinds of children's stories in relation to life and reading.

Introducing Books to Children AIDAN CHAMBERS (Heinemann, 1973) SBN 435 80261 5
An attempt to answer two critical problems: how to get children reading, and how to keep them reading. The author deals in a very common-sense way with the setting for reading, storytelling, the use of the library and setting up a school bookshop.

Library in the Primary School (School Library Association, 1966) SBN 900641 27 4
Although published over ten years ago, and therefore in some respects now out of date, this report is still very practical and effective.

Matters of Fact MARGERY FISHER (Hodder and Stoughton, 1972) SBN 340 03577 3
This is an analysis of children's information books, arranged by such topics as Bread, Abraham Lincoln, Journalism and London. There are important principles implied by this book.

Only Connect Edited by SHEILA EGOFF and others (Oxford University Press, 1969) SBN 19 540161 1
Subtitled 'readings on English Literature', this is a collection of articles chosen for their 'fresh, original and illuminating message'.

The Ordinary and the Fabulous ELIZABETH COOK (Oxford University Press, 2nd edition, 1975) SBN 521 09961 7
An introduction to myths, legends, and fairy tales for teachers and story-tellers, which examines the choice and presentation of different stories to listeners and readers between the ages of 8 and 14.

A Question of Reading: Organisation of Resources for Reading in Primary School CLIFF MOON and BRIDIE RABAN (Ward Lock, 1975) SBN 7062 3448 0

Detailed discussion and advice on how to organise the school
reading environment; suggests way of selecting, coding and
banding reading material.

A Sense of Story JOHN ROWE TOWNSEND (Kestrel, 1971) SBN 582
15467 6
A collection of essays about well known children's writers such as
Philippa Pearce, Helen Cresswell and Alan Garner.

Tales out of School GEOFFREY TREASE (Heinemann, 1964) SBN 435
80900 8
An affectionate but critical account of children's stories which
derives from a very wide knowledge of them.

Using Books in the Primary School (School Library Association, 1970)
SBN 900641 04 5
A report surveying the work of 70 schools where books have
played a major part in extending children's learning.

Written for Children JOHN ROWE TOWNSEND (Penguin, 1976) SBN 14
021920 X
An historical survey of children's books, written with a light
touch, and drawing attention especially to the tremendous boom
in children's books during the last twenty years.

ORGANISATION WITHIN THE LIBRARY

Dewey Decimal Classification for British Schools B. A. J. WINSLADE
(Forest Press Inc. for the School Library Association, in prepa-
ration 1977) [From Don Gresswell Ltd, Bridge House, Grange
Park, London, N21 1RB, for British schools.]
A revision of Marjorie Chambers' classification. Useful for large
school libraries only.

*Information in the School Library: Introduction to the Organisation of
Nonbook Materials* MALCOLM SHIFRIN (Bingley, 1973) SBN 85157
132 8
Many school book collections are being related to resource
centres, and this introduction to the topic also discusses that hoary
subject of central versus classroom collections.

School Libraries: Their Planning and Equipment (School Library
Association, 1972) SBN 900641 16 9
A practical book on planning and equipping school libraries.

BOOKSHOPS, BOOK CLUBS AND ORGANISATIONS

Owning books is a crucial experience for children. The setting up of a school bookshop has already been described (pages 00–00). The best advice is to be obtained by joining the School Bookshop Association; the School Bookshop Officer (7 Albemarle Street, London 4BB W1X—telephone: 01 493 9001) will supply the necessary information about this. The SBA has a travelling exhibition and will supply copies of *School Bookshop News*. They will also put you in touch with local booksellers who are willing to supply your school bookshop, usually on a sale-or-return basis.

Among the many shops and organisations that might be helpful are the following:

BOOKS FOR STUDENTS, Catteshall Lane, Godalming, Surrey, SU7 1NG
This organisation will run book fairs and exhibitions in schools; will supply school bookshops (the aim is to get books to schools within one week of ordering); and will also supply lockable display stands for school bookshops.

BOGLE-L'OUVERTURE, 5a Chignell Place, Ealing, London W13 9DU — telephone: 01 579 4920
Specialises in books from Africa, the Americas and the Caribbean.

BOOKSHOP, 121 Railton Road, London SE25
Specialises in Black literature.

BOOKWORM CLUB, Napier Place, Cumbernauld, Glasgow.
Similar to Scholastic Publications (q.v.), covering mainly the junior age range.

CENTERPRISE, 136 Kingsland High Street, London E8
As well as being a publisher of local people's writings this bookshop supplies school bookshops. It has large stocks of books from Africa, the Americas and the Caribbean, and material from other community publishing ventures.

CENTRE FOR LANGUAGE IN PRIMARY EDUCATION, Sutherland Street, London SW1 4LH — telephone: 01 828 4906
This is ILEA's principal teachers' centre for the study of language and literacy, running courses and study groups, disseminating information and helping individual schools and teachers. There is

a large permanent display of books and a member of staff is always available to advise visitors.

CHILDREN'S BOOK CENTRE, 229 Kensington High Street, London W8 6SA — telephone: 01 937 0862
One of the best displays of children's books to be seen in London. The shop will also organise school book exhibitions at which books are sold, but cannot stock school bookshops on a sale-or-return basis. For a small subscription, annotated book lists, etc., are sent regularly.

CHILDREN'S BOOK CLUB, Crossways, Hyde Road, Paignton, Devon
Similar to Scholastic Publications (q.v.). Though its list is shorter, its great advantage is that it lets children see sample copies before ordering.

CHILDREN'S RIGHTS WORKSHOP, 73 Balfour Street, London SE17
Non-establishment organisation commenting on racism, sexism, class, etc. in children's books. Issues lists.

INDEPENDENT PUBLISHING CO., 38 Kennington Lane, London SE11 — telephone: 01 735 2101
Indian material is a speciality, and this company will supply school bookshops. Stock lists are available and discounts are given to LEAs and schools.

NATIONAL BOOK LEAGUE, 7 Albemarle Street, London W1 4BB — telephone: 01 493 9001
Membership is cheap and beneficial, and there are frequent special exhibitions, often going on tour or on loan. The most important is the Children's Books of the Year Exhibition. In the basement is a permanent display of children's books published over the past twelve months. The Children's Book Officer is always available for advice and information.

NEW BEACON BOOKS, 76 Stroud Green Road, London N4 — telephone: 01 272 4889
Specialists in Caribbean literature and literature from developing countries; will help with a school exhibition.

PUFFIN SCHOOL BOOK CLUB, Penguin Books Ltd, Harmondsworth, Middlesex, UB7 0DA
Leaflets are distributed six times a year, describing a selection of Puffins.

SCHOLASTIC PUBLICATIONS LTD, 161 Fulham Road, London SW3 — telephone: 01 581 0241

There are book-clubs for pre-school and nursery level (*See-Saw*), infant (*Lucky*), junior (*Chip*) and secondary (*Scoop*). Newsletters are distributed six times a year with a selection of books for ordering.

THIRD WORLD PUBLICATIONS, 151 Stratford Road, Birmingham, B11 1RD

Imports material from Third World countries. Stock lists are available.

Acknowledgments

Contributions to this book were made by Judy Hargreaves (Beavers Holt Primary School, London SW15), Ken Mines (Princess May Junior School, London N16), Kate Austen (Kingsgate Infants School, London NW6) and Jane Herbert (Brunswick Park Infants School, London SE5).

All the photographs in this book have been taken by Keith Hawkins, Media Resources Officer, Ebury Teachers' Centre, London, in four ILEA primary schools (St Peter's CE Primary School, Hammersmith, London W6; Beatrix Potter Primary School, London SW18; Kingsgate Infants School, London NW6; and Brunswick Park Infants School, London SE5), and the editors and publisher would like to thank the staff and children of these schools for their cooperation.

The editors are most grateful to the Centre Secretary, Miss Doris Anstee, for her patience and care in typing and retyping the text.

The editors and publisher are also grateful to the following for permission to reprint copyright material in this book: Atheneum Publishers Inc., New York, for the poem 'Shadows', copyright © 1968 by Patricia Hubbell from *Catch Me a Wind* (used by permission of Atheneum Publishers); Andre Deutsch Ltd, London, for three passages from *Mind Your Own Business* by Michael Rosen; Harcourt Brace Jovanovich Inc., New York, for a verse from 'Why did the children' from *The People, Yes* by Carl Sandburg, copyright 1936 by Harcourt Brace Jovanovich Inc., copyright 1964 by Carl Sandburg (reprinted by permission of the publishers). The verse from the poem 'Loneliness' by Janet Pomeroy (page 43) is reproduced by kind permission of the *Daily Mirror* Children's Literary Competition.

Bibliographical index

Books* mentioned in the text (excluding those listed between pages 84 and 88)

*Paperback editions have usually been preferred

Frog and Toad Together World's Work (1973)   437 90089 4
    page 48, 73
Lollipops (from BREAKTHROUGH TO LITERACY) Longman Set of 4,
    582 19132 7   (may be bought as a single volume,
    582 15364 6)   *page 39*
Macaulay, David *Cathedral: The story of its construction* Collins (1974)
    00 19215o 9   *page 46*
        City: A story of Roman planning and construction Collins (1975)
    00 19215 7   *page 46, 74*
MACDONALD JUNIOR REFERENCE LIBRARY *The Motor Car*
    Macdonald (1968)   356 02419 9   *page 46*
MACDONALD STARTERS *Spiders* Macdonald (1971)   356 03846 7
    (and many other titles)   *page 49*
Mackay, David *The Loose Tooth* In BREAKTHROUGH BOOKS, Red Set
    A Longman (1970)   582 19053 3   *page 75*
        A Rainy Day In BREAKTHROUGH BOOKS, Yellow Set B
    Longman (1970)   582 19051 7   *page 31*
McKee, David *Six Men* A. and C. Black (1972)   7136 1343 2
    page 70
Manning-Sanders, Ruth *A Book of Princes and Princesses* Pan Books
    (1973)   330 23718 7   *page 36*
Matterson, Elizabeth *This Little Puffin: finger plays and nursery games*
    Penguin (1969)   14 030300 6   *page 39*
Maybury, Barry *Wordscapes* Oxford University Press (1970)
    19 83313 8 X   *page 53-4*
Mayne, William *No More School* Hamish Hamilton (1965)
    241 90485 4   *page 33*
Milligan, Spike *A Book of Milliganimals* Penguin (1971)
    14 03047 6 2   *page 41*
Milne, A. A. "Bad Sir Brian Botany" in *When we were Very Young*
    (first published 1924; reissued many times) Methuen (1965)
    416 22580 2   *page 42*
Mirsky, Reba *Thirty-one Brothers and Sisters* New York: Follett
    (1952) (Now out of print)   *page 59*
MONSTER BOOKS Four sets, each of 3 books Longman   *page 19*
            Set A   582 18642 0
            Set B   582 18643 9
            Set C   582 18644 7
            Set D   582 18645 5
Motor Car, The Ladybird (1965)   7214 0127 9   *page 46*
Nash, Ogden *The Animal Garden* Deutsch (1972)   233 96180 1
    page 42
Naughton, Bill *The Goalkeeper's Revenge* Penguin (1970)
    14 03034 8 0   *page 10, 31-2*